Contents

KU-607-318

Approximate walk times

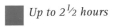 Up to 2½ hours   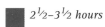 2½–3½ hours   4 hours and over

The walk times are provided as a guide only and are calculated using an average walking speed of 2½mph (4km/h), adding one minute for each 10m (33ft) of ascent, and then rounding the result to the nearest half hour.

Keymap

SCALE 1:277 777 or 1 INCH to about 4½ MILES *1CM to 2.7KM*

KILOMETRES

MILES

KEYMAP HEIGHTS SHOWN IN METRES

At-a-glance...

Walk	Page	Start	Nat. Grid Reference	Distance	Time	Height Gain
Alport Castles	81	Fairholmes National Park Centre	SK 172893	8¼ miles (13.3km)	4½ hrs	1,950ft (594m)
Beeley and Hob Hurst's House	53	Beeley	SK 265674	6¼ miles (10.1km)	3 hrs	950ft (290m)
Biggin and Biggin Dale	59	Alsop Moor	SK 157564	6½ miles (10.5km)	3½ hrs	1,310ft (399m)
Broomhead Reservoir	44	Bolsterstone	SK 270967	6 miles (9.7km)	3 hrs	1,000ft (305m)
Chee Dale	37	Miller's Dale	SK 138732	5¾ miles (9.3km)	3 hrs	1,290ft (393m)
Crowden and Millstone Rocks	65	Crowden	SK 072992	6½ miles (10.5km)	3½ hrs	1,550ft (472m)
Dane Bridge and Lud's Church	56	Gradbach	SJ 998662	6¼ miles (10.1km)	3 hrs	1,120ft (341m)
Deep Dale and the Magpie Mine	20	White Lodge	SK 170705	4¾ miles (7.6km)	2½ hrs	780ft (238m)
Dovestone Edge	78	Binn Green	SE 017043	9¼ miles (14.9km)	4½ hrs	1,750ft (533m)
Edale and Crookstone Hill	71	Edale	SK 123853	7¾ miles (12.5km)	4 hrs	1,700ft (518m)
Elton and Robin Hood's Stride	16	Elton	SK 221609	3¾ miles (6km)	2 hrs	730ft (223m)
Eyam and Stoney Middleton	12	Eyam	SK 216767	3½ miles (5.6km)	1½ hrs	660ft (201m)
Grindon and the River Hamps	68	Grindon	SK 085544	7½ miles (12.1km)	4 hrs	1,500ft (457m)
Higger Tor and Burbage Rocks	14	Upper Burbage Bridge	SK 260830	3¾ miles (6km)	2 hrs	720ft (219m)
Kinder Low	84	Hayfield	SK 036869	10½ miles (16.9km)	5½ hrs	2,180ft (664m)
Langsett and Midhope Reservoirs	62	Langsett Reservoir	SE 210004	6½ miles (10.5km)	3 hrs	950ft (290m)
Lord's Seat	28	Barber Booth	SK 107847	5½ miles (8.9km)	3 hrs	1,150ft (351m)
Lose Hill	47	Edale	SK 123853	6 miles (9.7km)	3½ hrs	1,650ft (503m)
Lyme Park and the Macclesfield Canal	50	Nelson Pit, Higher Poynton	SJ 944833	6¼ miles (10.1km)	3 hrs	625ft (191m)
Margery Hill	88	Fairholmes National Park Centre	SK 172893	11¼ miles (18.1km)	5½ hrs	2,000ft (610m)
Pilsbury Castle	31	Hartington	SK 128604	5½ miles (8.9km)	2½ hrs	830ft (253m)
Standedge Tunnel	40	Marsden	SE 047118	6 miles (9.7km)	3 hrs	950ft (290m)
The Chatsworth Estate	18	Baslow	SK 258722	4¼ miles (6.8km)	2 hrs	510ft (155m)
Warslow	26	Wetton Mill	SK 094560	5¼ miles (8.4km)	2½ hrs	970ft (296m)
Whinstone Lee Tor and Cutthroat Bridge	24	Ashopton lay-by beside A57	SK 196864	4¾ miles (7.7km)	2½ hrs	1,025ft (312m)
Win Hill and Hope Cross	74	Ashopton Heatherdene car park	SK 202858	8¼ miles (13.3km)	4 hrs	1,590ft (485m)
Win Hill and Thornhill	34	Ashopton Heatherdene car park	SK 202858	6¼ miles (10.1km)	3 hrs	1,350ft (411m)
Wormhill and Monk's Dale	22	Miller's Dale	SK 138732	4¾ miles (7.6km)	2½ hrs	920ft (280m)

Comments

The intriguing natural formations of Alport Castles result from instability of the shales at the edge of the Gritstone cap and are here reached from the neighbouring Derwent Valley.

Local folklore often attributed mysterious settings as the home of a hob, a malevolent elf. His home here is an unusual Bronze Age burial on the moor above the Chatsworth Estate.

The Tissington Trail and the less frequented Biggin Dale are paired on this enjoyable and relatively undemanding ramble that includes the village of Biggin whose pub makes a convenient part-way halt.

Although barely a mile (1.6km) from the Stocksbridge steel works, the Broomhead Valley is a world apart. Quiet woodlands by the lake contrast with airy hilltops on this pleasant round of the vale.

The narrow confines of Chee Dale leave no room for a footpath and the way through resorts to stepping stones along the bed of the stream, adding yet another dimension to this spectacular walk.

Once a royal hunting forest, Longdendale now holds a string of reservoirs. This impressive walk onto the crags above reveals some of the finest views along its length.

The higher reaches of the Dane Valley are forested in pine, fir and birch, concealing a deep gorge where the river tumbles over dark rocks. Hanging Stone, Lud's Church and grand views are other highlights.

Bumps crumpling the landscape are often all that remains of the lead mines of old, but at Magpie Mine tall chimneys, a ruined engine house and pit-head gear illustrate the extent of the workings.

The Dark Peak has no shortage of fine edge walks, but this one above the Dovestone reservoirs must rank among the most spectacular.

In a variation to the classic walk from Edale, this walk explores the south-eastern edge of the Kinder plateau, returning past old booths along the Vale of Edale.

A prehistoric stone circle, medieval hermit's cell, myths of Robin Hood and a beggar's 'mansion' add intrigue to this superb short walk through an eastern outcrop of the White Peak's gritstone.

A short ramble from Eyam to neighbouring Stoney Middleton passes many reminders of the 17th-century visitation by the plague as well as an unusual octagonal church.

The fact that, during the summer months, the River Hamps flows largely below the surface in no way detracts from the delightful scenery of its lower reaches where it meets the River Manifold.

Spectacular views and a fascinating prehistoric enclosure are highlights of this undemanding ramble.

Kinder Scout was once described as a grouse moor and the ascent is therefore on sufferance only. Nowadays this grand hike takes in two of its best features, the Kinder Downfall and Kinder Low.

A variation to the classic walk around the popular Langsett Reservoir, which takes in the neighbouring water of Midhope and its surrounding forest.

Lord's Seat provides the most dramatic ridge walk in the northern Peak, giving unrivalled prospects into Edale and across the limestone plateau to the south.

Gifted to G.H.B. Ward, one of the prime activists for access onto the moor, Lose Hill has assumed iconic status and marks the culmination of one of the finest ridge walks in the Peak.

The Macclesfield Canal brought the industrial age to the Peak's western fringe, here serving coal mines now overgrown as nature reserves. The walk provides an alternative approach to the Lyme Park estate.

The highest point overlooking the Derwent Valley is to be found among the undulations of Margery Hill, whose relative remoteness emphasises the stark beauty of these northern moors.

Despite the lack of turreted battlements and vaulted undercrofts, Pilsbury is one of the most spectacular early Norman castle sites, reached here from the attractive former market town of Hartington.

Combine a unique trip through the deepest, highest, longest canal tunnel in the country with a satisfying walk back across the moors.

Regarded as one of the 'Wonders of the Peak', Chatsworth House ranks amongst the finest mansions in the country. This is an enjoyable stroll through the extensive estate.

Beginning by the National Trust-owned Wetton Mill and tearoom, this walk explores one of the lesser known paths in the Manifold Valley, a delightful old lane following its eastern flank.

A roundabout route through a woodland nature reserve and across the moors offers a leisurely approach to the spectacular views of Derwent Edge.

The long, broad tail of Win Hill reveals a changing perspective across the valleys of the Ashop and the Noe. The walk returns beside the western arm of the Ladybower Reservoir.

Win Hill's craggy summit demands an energetic walk from almost every direction, but the ascent via Thornhill lessens the gradient and gives a superb view into Upper Derwent.

The woodlands crowding the Monk's Dale Nature Reserve conceal a wealth of wildlife, while Miller's Dale reveals the extent of the 19th-century limestone industry instigated by the railways.

At-a-glance...

Introduction to the Peak District

Introduction

The area known as the Peak encompasses the southern extremity of the Pennine uplift, the longest contiguous range of hills in the country, which runs from the Scottish borders all the way to the Midland plains. Much of the Peak falls within Derbyshire, but the hills over-spill into the counties of Yorkshire, Staffordshire, Cheshire and Greater Manchester too. Despite a relatively compact size, barely 40 miles (64km) from top to bottom and only 20 miles (32km) wide, it embodies vividly contrasting landscapes, their disparate characters springing from the bedrock upon which they lie. The highest land is to be found in the north and is footed on gritstone, a hard impermeable sandstone that weathers almost to black. It gives rise to vast rolling moors abruptly bounded by dark, dramatically weatherworn cliffs known as 'edges'. Farther south, the gritstone runs out in two peripheral horns that embrace a lower, grassy limestone plateau, neatly partitioned by miles of drystone walls and riven by pretty dales and deep gorges, which grace the area with much of its beauty.

The word 'peak' might conjure an image of dramatic pinnacles and lofty heights, perhaps attained only after the effort of a scramble. But here you will find few craggy summits or prodigious heights, the greatest elevation of 2,088 feet (636m) being barely distinguishable amid an unrelieved wilderness on the Kinder plateau.

The National Park

Despite the lack of 'peaks', this is grand walking country and was appreciated as such long before the National Park came into existence. By the close of the 19th century, industrial expansion was pushing at the edge of the moors and many factory workers looked to the clear, open spaces on their doorstep for recreation; a chance to escape the crowding, noise and dirt of their workaday lives. However, most of the land was private, preserved as grouse moors, sheep runs or water catchment for the numerous reservoirs being built in the higher valleys. Many viewed this blanket prohibition as a deep injustice and braved the often-aggressive gamekeepers to practise the 'gentle art of trespass'. Ramblers' groups and footpath preservation societies achieved some success in opening Rights of Way, yet the Kinder Trespass in 1932 was a milestone. Although neither the first nor the last mass trespass, it became iconic, partly because of its scale, some 500 people took to the moor, but also for the harshness of punishment meted out to the handful of ringleaders arrested. This turned the tide of public sympathy and developed a will to change the law, which eventually led to the enactment of the *National Park and Access to the Countryside Act* in 1949 and subsequently, *the Countryside and Rights of Way Act* in 2000.

The Peak District National Park was created in 1951 as a direct result of the 1949 Act, the first of its kind in Britain. In relation to its size, 555 square miles (1,437km²), it is the second most visited in the country, not surprising since roughly half of England's

Dropping from Higger Tor to Carl Wark

population is calculated to live within a couple of hours' drive. Yet, despite this proximity to so many people, the park has only one settlement, Bakewell, that can be called a town, and huge tracts of the Peak remain totally unspoiled. Its most famous beauty spots are justifiably popular and are best avoided on a summer's weekend. But with 124 square miles (321km²) of open access land and 1,867 miles (3,005km) of designated Rights of Way, it is possible even on the busiest bank holiday to spend a day on the hills or in the valleys and hardly see a soul.

The Dark and White Peaks

The disparate regions of grit and limestone have engendered the convenient labels of 'Dark' and 'White', a distinction that cannot properly be accommodated within practicalities of map production. The geological boundary between them is as abrupt as that suggested by the linear demarcation of the two Ordnance Survey Explorer sheets covering the area, but in reality describes a great arc that has Castleton at its apex. So, while the area of the northern sheet is almost entirely founded upon grit and sandstones, the country charted upon the southern sheet is underlain by both types of rock.

The high, wilderness landscape of the Dark Peak has little habitation with few roads or tracks crossing, and, apart from the lower slopes, it is unsuitable for intensive agriculture and thus largely unfettered by physical boundaries. But, although its very inhospitability served to check the growth of the manufacturing towns that spawned along its peripheral valleys, the vast moorland, in a way, was a reason for their very existence. The emergence of the industrial age demanded power to drive the factory machines, something freely available in the abundant streams that cascaded off the heights along the deep cloughs. Bold engineers overcame the remoteness from seaports with the construction, first of canals and later railways to bring in raw materials and take away the finished goods. As the towns grew, so did their need for water and the Victorian city fathers turned to the brooding hills, damming the upper valleys to create vast reservoirs. It was here too that they found the stone for their great buildings and countless quarries large and small were cut into the hillsides. The hard, coarse stone found in some areas was particularly suited for use as millstones, which were of such high quality that an export trade even developed. Their importance to the area is reflected in the fact that a millstone is adopted by the National Park as its emblem.

Abandoned quarries mimic the high weatherworn escarpments or edges that fringe the upland plateau, the most obviously dramatic feature of these rugged hills. Forest and woodland planting around many of the reservoir lakes has softened their shores and Nature has been quick to adapt to the changing conditions, birdlife in particular exploiting many of the new opportunities created.

The overriding character of the Dark Peak is that of undulating upland moor, an all but featureless and seemingly limitless expanse. Sparse grasses, spike rush, cotton grass, heathers and bilberry are the plants to be found here, while the poorly drained tops are often covered by peat bog that has been eroded into a bizarre landscape of groughs (the deep troughs and channels) and hags (black islands of peat not yet washed out). Itinerant sheep appear totally ignorant of their solitude and, the only other life to be seen here are the birds. Red grouse are common, indeed much of the heather moorland is specifically managed for their benefit.

In sharp contrast, the great dome of Carboniferous limestone to the south is criss-crossed by lanes and peppered with the settlement of farms, hamlets and characterful villages. Miles of drystone walling neatly partition the countryside into fields and meadows, grazed by cattle where the grass is richest with sheep roaming elsewhere. The high, undulating plateau is fractured by a web of deep gorges that radiate from its heart, cut by torrential glacial melt-water rivers at the end of the Ice Age. But this is karst country and in many places the river now flows deep beneath the ground leaving some dales completely dry while in others the water flows only intermittently. Such a landscape is riddled with caves, sometimes little more than a hollow, but elsewhere great, gaping yawns delving deep into the ground.

However, not all the subterranean passages are due to nature, for the Peak's limestone is richly veined in metal ores, in particular lead and copper. Deeper mining on an industrial scale only became possible with the development of steam engines, employed to pump out water and haul the ore to the surface. Quarrying, too, suddenly became a major industry at the same time, the railways providing the key to cost effective operation. Although quarrying continues in a handful of places, mining has finished and only subtle traces of the area's industrial heritage remain upon the landscape.

Relative inaccessibility has protected the White Peak from obtrusive development and, away from the few main roads, its many lanes are narrow and comparatively quiet. Picturesque stone cottages cluster around a church and pub often belying the village's former importance as a market centre for lead and wool.

The walks

Many of the Dark Peak routes are focussed upon reservoirs, valleys and the edges of the moors. Elsewhere, the vast, featureless spaces may appear intimidating to the inexperienced. However, most described walks follow discernible paths, which, in fine weather, should present no great difficulty to the sensible novice. The longer moorland walks do present a challenge and newcomers to rambling would be advised to develop their experience on the less demanding routes first. On the limestone, few places are remote from a small village or the web of narrow lanes and tracks and general navigation is not a significant problem. However, countryside walking often demands attention to detail. Much of this part of the Peak is actively farmed and with fewer swathes of open access land, it is important to stick to the recognised paths.

Be aware that weather conditions on any high ground can be markedly different from those in the valleys and can very rapidly deteriorate. Adequate clothing and provisions and the ability to navigate using map and compass are necessary. It is easy to become disoriented in mist and in empty terrain, a GPS receiver can be a useful additional tool to pinpoint your position. Even in the sheltered dales, walking can be demanding for although climbs and descents may be relatively short, they are often abrupt. In the most popular gorges, good paths have been laid, but elsewhere the terrain is often rocky and, in wet conditions, limestone polished by the passage of innumerable feet and steep grass slopes can become very slippery.

This collection has been chosen to explore the many different aspects of the countryside and sometimes include or lie close to another attraction. The Park Authority does an excellent job in maintaining paths, stiles and gates. In most places, well-behaved dogs are welcome and ought to be kept on leads near livestock, in farmyard areas and while passing through nature reserves. They should also be restrained during the spring nesting season upon the moor and note also that, in some open access areas, dogs are not permitted other than on rights of way.

This book includes a list of waypoints alongside the description of the walk, so that you can enjoy the full benefits of gps should you wish to.
For more information on using your gps, read the *Pathfinder® Guide GPS for Walkers*, by gps teacher and navigation trainer, Clive Thomas (ISBN 978-0-7117-4445-5). For essential information on map reading and basic navigation, read the *Pathfinder® Guide Map Reading Skills* by outdoor writer, Terry Marsh (ISBN 978-0-7117-4978-8). Both titles are available in bookshops or can be ordered online at www.totalwalking.co.uk

Eyam and Stoney Middleton

		GPS waypoints
Start	Eyam	🗺 SK 216 767
Distance	3½ miles (5.6km)	Ⓐ SK 220 763
Height gain	660 feet (201m)	Ⓑ SK 226 758
Approximate time	1½ hours	Ⓒ SK 231 754
Parking	Car park opposite Eyam Museum (Pay and Display)	Ⓓ SK 234 759
		Ⓔ SK 228 763
Route terrain	Field paths and tracks	
Ordnance Survey maps	Landranger 119 (Buxton & Matlock), Explorer OL24 (The Peak District – White Peak area)	

Despite the sustained pull from Stoney Middleton, this is a pleasant walk, taking in some of Eyam's plague sites as well as an unusual church in the neighbouring village. The high ground enables some fine views across the Derwent Valley while the woodland sections proffer wild flowers in spring and shade in summer.

🗺 From the car park, walk down the hill and go left past Eyam Hall and the church. At a fork, bear left to stay with Church Street into the heart of the village. Cross The Square and turn right by the red telephone box into Lydgate Ⓐ.

Where it splits at the end, keep ahead through a gate beside cottages, the way signed to Stoney Middleton via the Boundary Stone.

Leaving Eyam behind, cross a couple of fields before picking up an old, walled track. Subsequently emerging into open pasture, keep going to find the Boundary Stone beside the path near a stand of trees Ⓑ. The dreaded plague reached Eyam in 1665, unwittingly brought in a bolt of cloth. The villagers bravely shut themselves off, preventing its wider spread, but condemning themselves to a horror in which two-thirds of the community perished. Neighbouring villagers left food at this boundary stone, the curious

holes in the top filled with vinegar to disinfect money left for payment. But Eyam had otherwise to fend for itself; nursing its sick and burying the dead. Despite such close contact, some miraculously survived. Elizabeth Hancock of Riley Farm buried her husband and six children within just a week, their graves collected in a hillside enclosure passed at the end of the walk.

The path falls towards Stoney Middleton past the craters of old bell mines that followed an outcrop of lead ore. Reaching a lane, walk into the village and go left along a back street. Where that shortly swings right towards the main road Ⓒ, branch left along The Nook towards St Martin's Church.

Dedicated to St Martin, the patron of soldiers and cripples, the church has an unusual octagonal nave. It was erected in 1757 following a fire in the medieval church, which had been endowed by Joan Eyre in thanksgiving for the safe return of her husband from Agincourt.

Light streams from the lantern upon inward facing pews, generating a sense of oneness. The font, intended as the centrepiece, links the rite of Christian baptism with the warm-water springs rising near the church, which have been known for at least two millennia and are credited with curative properties.

Curving left in front of the churchyard, the lane soon degrades to a track, climbing from the village past the extension cemetery. An old packhorse trail, it winds steeply into Stoney Woods, ultimately rising to the bend of a lane, New Road **D**. Cross to a gated track diagonally opposite and continue up the hillside, passing through gorse heath into more woodland. At a junction near the top, go left. The track then veers right above a high bank overlooking Middleton Dale. Breaking from the wood, join a tarmac drive, which shortly leads down past the Riley Graves; they lie within a small stone enclosure, over a stile in a field on the right **E**. Continue downhill through

The Boundary Stone

Riley Wood to a road at the bottom. Turn right back to Eyam and the car park.

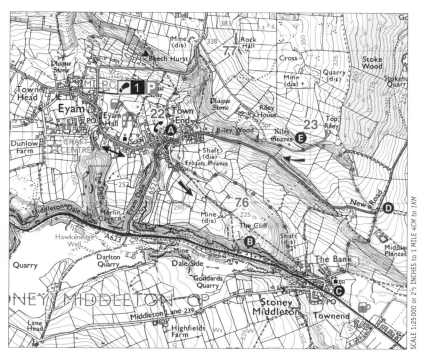

Higger Tor and Burbage Rocks

Start	Upper Burbage Bridge	**GPS waypoints**	
Distance	3¾ miles (6km)	🥾 SK 260 830	
Height gain	720 feet (219m)	Ⓐ SK 256 820	
Approximate time	2 hours	Ⓑ SK 258 815	
Parking	Car park west of bridge	Ⓒ SK 262 805	
Route terrain	Occasionally bouldery, but clear moorland paths	Ⓓ SK 270 815	
Ordnance Survey maps	Landranger 110 (Sheffield & Huddersfield), Explorer OL1 (The Peak District – Dark Peak area)		

Although short and undemanding, this circuit around the head of Burbage Brook lacks for nothing in stunning scenery. The route climbs over the spectacular viewpoint of Higger Tor to a second dramatic outcrop, long held to be a prehistoric fort. The return follows a superb edge overlooking the eastern side of the valley.

🥾 Begin from the small car park to the west of Upper Burbage Bridge, from which two paths are signed through a small gate. The higher one contours the slope of Fiddler's Elbow above the valley, undulating towards your first objective, the flat-topped hill of Higger Tor Ⓐ.

Bouldery on top and flanked by rocky buttresses, the platform offers a panorama across the Derwent Valley and the deep rift cradling Burbage Brook.

Descend from the southern tip to a clear path across Hathersage Moor, which leads onto the promontory of Carl Wark Ⓑ. Projecting above the valley it is a natural citadel secured by a high boulder and earth rampart that incorporates a defended gateway below the south-eastern corner. Nearby burial mounds, cairns and dwelling platforms indicate settlement since

From Higger Tor to the head of the Burbage Valley

the Bronze Age, but the true purpose of Carl Wark remains a mystery. Neighbouring forts on Mam Tor and at Navio suggest a military purpose, but today's historians argue that Higger Tor would then have been the more logical site. Limited excavations in 1950 failed to reveal decisive evidence and modern thinking favours a protective retreat for livestock and people in times of trouble.

Leave the enclosure at the far end of the wall, from which the ongoing path falls away across a bouldery slope. After breasting another lower outcrop, the path drops to the road beside Burbage Bridge. Crossing the bridge, follow the road up to a small car park **C**.

For an undemanding return, take the broad track from the back of the car park, which contours the valley side below the cliffs of Burbage Rocks. Known as the Duke's Drive, it led up to the grouse moors from the Duke of Rutland's shooting retreat, Longshaw Lodge, which is now owned by the National Trust.

However, the more interesting route follows a path along the top of the escarpment and is signposted to the right from beside the car park entrance. Through a small gate onto the open moor, head up the slope towards the ridge. Keep right where the path shortly forks, later passing a stone block, abandoned after it cracked while being fashioned into a water trough.

The path gains the top of the scar above an old quarry, suddenly revealing an impressive view across the valley, and continues along the rim, gently rising to the high point directly opposite Carl Wark. From here, its position appears even more impregnable, despite its subordination to Higger Tor. The cliffs then run out and the way descends, curving left to a junction by a waymark and cairn **D**.

Keep ahead, losing height to ford a stream before climbing once more to the continuing line of cliffs. The airy walk finally comes to an end as both path and lower track meet the lane beside Upper Burbage Bridge. ●

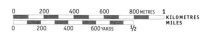

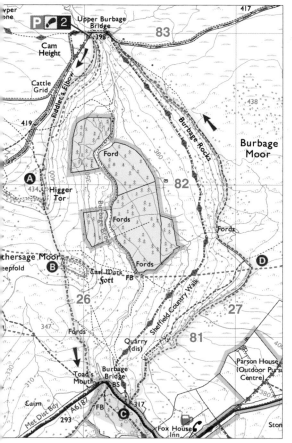

Elton and Robin Hood's Stride

		GPS waypoints	
Start	Elton		
Distance	3¾ miles (6km)	SK 221 609	
Height gain	730 feet (223m)	**A** SK 218 629	
		B SK 224 629	
Approximate time	2 hours	**C** SK 225 623	
Parking	Roadside parking in village	**D** SK 229 613	
Route terrain	Heath and field paths		
Ordnance Survey maps	Landranger 119 (Buxton & Matlock), Explorer OL24 (The Peak District – White Peak area)		

Although founded on limestone and surrounded by old lead workings, Elton looks across to striking outcrops of gritstone. The hill of an Iron Age fort, a prehistoric stone circle and medieval hermit's cave are also passed on this enjoyable countryside walk.

From the **Duke of York**, facing the church, go left and immediately right along a descending lane beside the graveyard. Bear left at a fork onto a track signed to Youlgreave, but as it swings right, leave through a small gate on the left. Walk to a signpost at the

The 12th-century rock shrine in the Hermitage

end of a hedge and turn right. Head down the fields, cross a stream and, over a stile, bear right on a rising trod that emerges onto Cliff Lane.

Take the stile opposite, climb to the field above and go right beside the fence. Walk beyond the corner to the crest and, over another stile, maintain the line to intercept a track. Continue forward towards an enclosed wood, skirting its boundary to the left. Passing through a gate keep going, eventually joining a field track. Ahead, it runs below Castle Ring Hill, soon reaching a junction of paths **A**.

Slip through a gate on the right and go left to a kissing-gate. Passing into mixed woodland, the path curves through the trees before emerging onto a lane **B**. Heading uphill, the distinctive outcrop of Robin Hood's Stride soon appears. Leave through a gate opposite the entrance to Harthill Moor Farm, following the Limestone

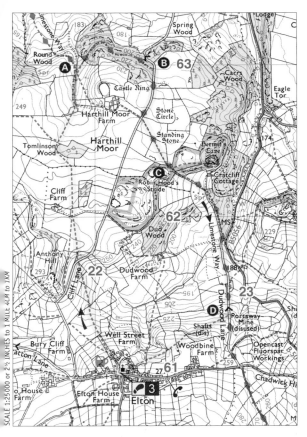

SCALE 1:25 000 or 2½ INCHES to 1 MILE 4CM to 1KM

| 0 | 200 | 400 | 600 | 800 METRES | 1 |
| 0 | 200 | 400 | 600 YARDS | ½ |

KILOMETRES
MILES

A prodigious leap, never mind a stride, would be necessary to pass between the two pinnacles of Robin Hood's Stride spaced some 50 feet (15m) apart. However, they are favourite challenges for rock climbers, who have dubbed them 'Weasel' and 'Inaccessible'. Seen in half-light from the south, the outcrop has the look of a turreted mansion, which gives it its other name of 'Mock Beggars' Hall'. Cratcliff Tor is also a haunt for climbers, who develop their skills among the chaos of boulders.

Readily accessible, though, is the 'Hermit's Cave', which is tucked below the eastern cliff. Now protected by a metal grill, it was the secluded cell of a 12th-century religious ascetic who left his mark in a crucifix cut into the living rock.

Return to the track and follow it downhill, carrying on at the edge of a field to join a track from Cratcliff Cottage. Meeting a narrow lane, walk up the hill for some 600 yds to locate a footpath signed over a stile on the right **D**. Head across the slope of the field to continue above an outgrown hedge. A developing trod curves over a shoulder to bring Elton into view. Keep heading towards the church, eventually leaving the fields beside a cottage. Walk through the churchyard opposite back to the village centre. ●

Way towards the eruption of rocks. In a field over to the left are four upright stones of a Bronze Age circle, one of several to be found in the area. Through a gate at the foot of Robin Hood's Stride, the onward path lies over a stile to the left **C**, but first you might explore the rocks.

Having crossed the stile, briefly follow the track right to find another stile on the left. Climb the field to a second outcrop of bouldery rocks, Cratcliff Tor. Although partly shrouded by woodland, these are equally impressive and conceal an intriguing stone shelter, which you will find at the base of the cliffs in the trees around to the right.

The Chatsworth Estate

Start	Baslow		GPS waypoints
Distance	4¼ miles (6.8km)		✎ SK 258 722
Height gain	510 feet (155m)		Ⓐ SK 258 718
Approximate time	2 hours		Ⓑ SK 269 717
Parking	At start off A619 (Pay and Display)		Ⓒ SK 265 706
			Ⓓ SK 268 704
Route terrain	Parkland, woodland paths and tracks, steep stepped descent		Ⓔ SK 263 703
			Ⓕ SK 257 702
Ordnance Survey maps	Landranger 119 (Buxton & Matlock), Explorer OL24 (The Peak District – White Peak area)		

Chatsworth is one of Britain's most renowned palatial mansions and can be visited on this undemanding walk from the neighbouring village of Baslow. The route explores part of the extensive park and woodland surrounding the hall, passing a striking hilltop hunting tower, all that remains of the original 16th-century Cavendish house.

✎ Turn right out of the car park and keep ahead at the bend to cross a bridge spanning Bar Brook. A track is then signed right past a thatched terrace to Chatsworth. Entering the estate, wind around Plantation Cottage into the park. Immediately through the gate Ⓐ, leave the path and go sharp left, following a sign to Robin Hood. Beyond the corner of a high fence bounding a small wood, strike almost due east across the open park, intersecting a drive from Park Lodge. Beyond a second track, clamber over a stile in an intervening fence, the ground then rising towards the high terrain of Dobb Edge. Approaching a wood, skirt it to the left, shortly coming upon a bracken-filled gully, which serves as a guide to the top of the hill Ⓑ.

Turn right beside a wall above Dobb Edge. Reaching a stile, cross into a plantation and go left to find a broad track. To the right, it runs beside the wood, later becoming metalled as another track joins from the left. At a second junction Ⓒ, go left, walking gently uphill for ¼ mile to Emperor Lake Ⓓ. The 8-acre (3.2-hectare) lake was created in 1844 to supply the Emperor Fountain, which, on a good day, can spout water 280 feet (85m) into the air.

Retrace your steps along the track, but just before reaching Ⓒ, branch left to the Hunting Tower. The Cavendish line at Chatsworth began when Bess of Hardwick persuaded her second husband William to settle in her native Derbyshire. They bought Chatsworth in 1549 and built a grand Elizabethan house. Since demolished and rebuilt by their descendants, only this tower remains, from which the womenfolk watched the hunt.

Drop beyond the tower to a drive and cross to a path opposite into the dense rhododendron of Stand Wood. It soon turns straight down the hillside beside a stream, *demanding care as the steps are steep and sometimes slippery.* Crossing the brook, the path turns out to an estate track, continuing diagonally opposite and descending to yet another drive **E**. Now turn right, past the entrance of the farmyard (where the animals and adventure playground are a particular delight for younger visitors) to the main car park, beside which is the entrance to the hall and gardens.

When Celia Fiennes visited in 1697, the newly created First Duke of Devonshire, William Cavendish was completing his bold architectural masterpiece. She delighted in the mansion's grandeur as had Thomas Hobbes before her, tutor and companion to the duke's father, the third Earl. In fact Hobbes was so impressed he waxed lyrical in Latin verse and included it

The Hunting Tower was built in Bess of Hardwick's day

within his 'Wonders of the Peak' – *de Mirabilibus Pecci.* Successive generations have added to the house, its furnishings and gardens, now invested within a charitable trust to ensure public enjoyment for generations to come.

Continue down to the ornamental bridge, built in 1762 **F**. Remaining on this bank, head upstream past Queen Mary's Bower. The way soon moves from the river to skirt the walled nursery and White Lodge. Where the drive swings across Bar Brook, keep ahead on a path to the revolving gate by which you entered the park. ●

Deep Dale and the Magpie Mine

		GPS waypoints
Start	White Lodge at foot of Taddington Dale	 SK 170 705
Distance	4¾ miles (7.6km)	Ⓐ SK 169 702
Height gain	780 feet (238m)	Ⓑ SK 158 685
		Ⓒ SK 166 681
Approximate time	2½ hours	Ⓓ SK 172 681
Parking	Car park beside A6 at start (Pay and Display)	Ⓔ SK 173 687
		Ⓕ SK 173 692
Route terrain	Field paths, tracks, steep descent	Ⓖ SK 169 695
Ordnance Survey maps	Landranger 119 (Buxton & Matlock), Explorer OL24 (The Peak District – White Peak area)	

One of several Deep Dales, this climbs from the Wye Valley onto the limestone plateau. The area was heavily mined for lead and the walk leads past one of the best-preserved mines in the country. Open views accompany the return from Sheldon, which concludes in a steep descent at the edge of Great Shacklow Wood.

Follow a path from the payment machine across the adjoining picnic area to a gate. Carry on over another meadow, ignoring a path off to Taddington to meet a stream. Follow it up a short distance, crossing to a stile. Head away on a winding path that leads to a junction at the foot of Deep Dale Ⓐ, where Deep Dale and Monyash are signed to the right. The path soon rejoins the stream crossed earlier, following it effortlessly into the valley.

Reconstructed horse gin

Keep going along the shallowing dale to a gate. Slip through to continue on the other side, eventually emerging onto a broad track. Go left to a lane Ⓑ. To the left it runs dead straight for almost ½ mile towards the Magpie workings, whose attendant buildings appear in distant view. Ignore the Sheldon turn-off, but leave at the bottom of the dip Ⓒ for a path, which crosses the fields to the main pit head.

Today, the shell of a massive engine house and stout round chimney dominate the mine, which was worked for over 200 years until final closure in 1954. Flooding was an ever-present problem, temporarily solved with the introduction of early Cornish steam pumps. But they were unable to cope with the deepening workings and eventually, a mile (1.6km) long drainage sough was dug to the River Wye below Great Shacklow Wood.

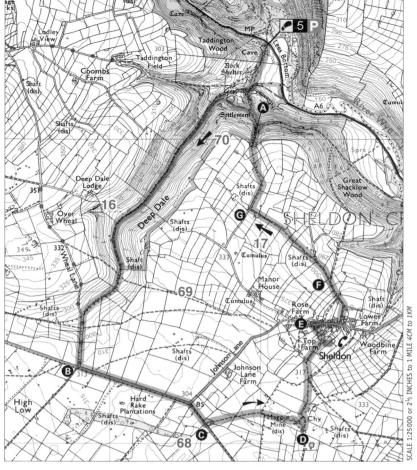

SCALE 1:25000 or 2½ INCHES to 1 MILE 4CM to 1KM

0	200	400	600	800 METRES	1
					KILOMETRES
					MILES
0	200	400	600 YARDS	½	

At a junction in front of the manager's cottage **D** go left (north), passing the circular ruin of the powder house, prudently distanced from all else in case of accident. Bear left to a stile in the corner and continue across an open field. Following a sign to Sheldon, carry on across a second field and then go right along a broad, walled track. Keep by the right wall beyond its end and in the next field swing left to a stile behind a corrugated barn. Cross to another stile by a small dew pond and walk through to emerge onto the main village street **E**.

Turn right past the **Cock and Pullet** but leave just beyond along a track on the left, signed to the church. Ignoring a junction, carry on for nearly ¼ mile, keeping an eye open for a stile on the left from which a path is signed to

White Lodge and Deep Dale **F**. Head across to a second stile and stay by the wall, maintaining the same direction across subsequent fields. Eventually the way becomes contained past the hummocks of more mining activity to meet the end of a track **G**. Go right, and in the second field, slip across the wall to continue on its opposite flank. Towards the bottom, veer to a gate into the Deep Dale Nature Reserve. The ongoing path drops very steeply at the edge of Great Shacklow Wood. Meeting a lower path emerging from a wicket gate, walk left, the way falling more easily to the junction at Point **A**. Retrace your outward steps to the White Lodge car park. ●

Wormhill and Monk's Dale

		GPS waypoints
Start	Miller's Dale	🥾 SK 138 732
Distance	4¾ miles (7.6km)	Ⓐ SK 130 733
Height gain	920 feet (280m)	Ⓑ SK 127 734
Approximate time	2½ hours	Ⓒ SK 123 742
Parking	Car park at former station (Pay and Display)	Ⓓ SK 130 753
		Ⓔ SK 141 733
Route terrain	Field and uneven rocky paths through woodland	
Ordnance Survey maps	Landranger 119 (Buxton & Matlock), Explorer OL24 (The Peak District – White Peak area)	

From the Monsal Trail at the foot of Chee Dale, the walk climbs to the pretty hamlet of Wormhill, passing its attractive manor and small church. After following an old lane across the fields, the route returns through the delightful National Nature Reserve of Monk's Dale.

🥾 Follow the Monsal Trail from the old platforms of Miller's Dale Station west towards Chee Dale and Buxton. As you approach a viaduct spanning the Wye, the Monsal Trail is signed off right Ⓐ down a stepped path to the river below. Follow the riverbank upstream to a junction by a bridge at the foot of Chee Dale Ⓑ. Leaving the river, turn through a gate and follow an inclined path to Wormhill. Entering a meadow, curve right over the shoulder of the hill and climb along a narrow, wooded side-valley above a stream. Through a gate, continue past a cottage to emerge onto a lane. Head uphill past Wormhill Hall to the tiny village, there turning off along a side lane to the church Ⓒ.

Wormhill lay within the Royal Forest, where poaching was not the only threat to game and during the 14th century, a certain John Wolfhurt held land in return for hunting wolves out. The church, originally a chapel of ease to Tideswell, contains a memorial to James

Brindley, a local lad who established his reputation as an engineer in building the Bridgewater Canal.

Degrading to a track, the lane swings left. Leave just past a cottage along a short, contained path on the left. Keep ahead across successive narrow fields to meet a walled track and follow it right. It meanders between the fields for ½ mile to end in a sloping pasture. Accompany the onward hedge to a waymark and there bear left to a gate at the bottom onto a lane. Walk down to a stile in the dip on the right Ⓓ, and head across the pasture into the narrow confines of Monk's Dale.

Now dry, the upper gorge shelters a dense ash wood, whose dank, mossy understorey is rich in spring wildflowers. Lower down, the stream resurges and the valley opens to steep meadows on either side. Originally held by the Cluniac priory of Lenton, trouble arose during the 13th century after King John sought to sweeten the Bishop of

Coventry and Lichfield by gifting him the endowment. Lenton's protests were ignored until the monks took up arms and seized tithes stored in Tideswell church. Despite papal intervention, the dispute continued for three centuries until all became confiscated under Henry VIII's Dissolution.

Eventually breaking from the trees, the path continues across scrub meadow, rewarding a climb across the valley side with a superb view along the dale. Later passing back into woodland, the path drops to a bridge spanning the stream. Rising into the corner of a meadow, stay by the wall to a stile from which a twisting path descends to emerge beside the church **E**. Cross to the narrow lane opposite, signed to Litton Mill. Just past the site of an old corn mill and before reaching the **Angler's Rest**, turn off along a

Wormhill Hall and its grounds from the lane

waymarked path on the right, which crosses the mill leat and then the River Wye. Climb left to the embankment of the former railway and follow it right, back to Miller's Dale Station. ●

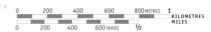

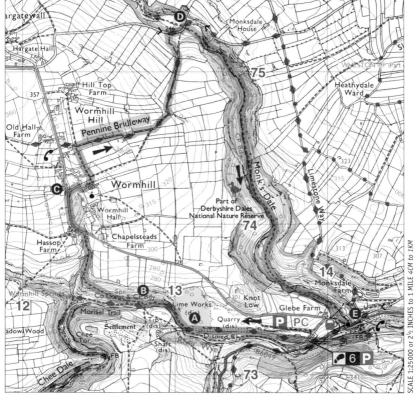

Whinstone Lee Tor and Cutthroat Bridge

		GPS waypoints
Start	Ashopton – lay-by beside A57	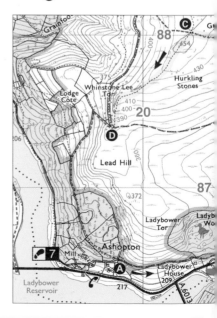 SK 196 864
Distance	4¾ miles (7.7km)	**Ⓐ** SK 198 865
Height gain	1,025 feet (312m)	**Ⓑ** SK 220 878
Approximate time	2½ hours	**Ⓒ** SK 203 880
Parking	Lay-by beside A57 at the start	**Ⓓ** SK 197 874
Route terrain	Generally good moorland paths, but *take care in mist*	
Ordnance Survey maps	Landranger 110 (Sheffield & Huddersfield), Explorer OL1 (The Peak District – Dark Peak area)	

Tackled from Derwent, the Derwent Edge demands a strenuous climb. But this roundabout route above Ladybower Brook and the moor behind the scarp adopts a more leisurely approach. Stunning views accompany the return past the southern-most of the outcrops, for which the edge is famous.

This enjoyable walk revels in splendid scenery and passes through one of the Peak District's few remaining oak woods. This was once the predominant vegetation of the northern Peak and in the sloping shelter of the valley, there is a rich variety of plant life, including mosses, lichens and ferns. Limestone erupts just to the south, but here the hills are gritstone, their exposed tops cloaked in peat and heather moor that is home to red grouse. The lack of cover also encourages predators such as peregrine and merlin, which hover motionless in the wind before swooping down upon their prey. And, if your luck is really in, you might also see a mountain hare.

🦶 From the parking area, walk towards the viaduct spanning the northern arm of the Ladybower Reservoir. Just before, cross to a rising tarmac drive and follow it around a sharp bend. Through a gate continue to the end, where a path is signed to Cutthroat Bridge through a small gate ahead **Ⓐ**.

Contouring the bracken-clad hillside, there is a fine view to the Ladybower Dam before passing into woodland. Meeting a track rising from the **Ladybower Inn**, follow it up the hill and through a gate into the Ladybower Woods Nature Reserve. When the track splits, branch right, shortly fording a small brook cascading down the hill. Carry on to another fork above Cutthroat Bridge.

Keep ahead, clambering down to negotiate a stream. The path then wanders easily across the hillside eventually leading to a ladder-stile. Just beyond, is an ancient milestone, marking the old road to Sheffield.

Passing through a field-gate **B**, immediately turn left on a track rising beside a wall and signed to Derwent via Derwent Edge. Scale a stile by a second gate higher up and continue across the open heather moor. After dipping to re-cross the stream encountered earlier the path rises to a fork by a T-shaped grouse butt. Bear left and carry on up

Dropping below Lead Hill

the hill, later passing a lone standing stone beside the path before you finally broach the ridge to encounter a crossing path **C**.

The onward route lies to the left, but it is worth first wandering a little way along the path ahead for the view into the upper Derwent Valley and along the edge past the Wheel Stones to White Tor. Heading south from the junction, the path gradually loses height past the Hurkling Stones and Whinstone Lee Tor. After a while you reach another crossing of paths **D** beside a small promontory overlooking the foot of the lake, a further opportunity to dally while enjoying the superb vista.

The way down lies along the footpath to the right, not the bridleway leaving sharp right. It falls steeply through a rocky cleft before sweeping left across a bracken slope to then run beside a wall. The dramatic views are eventually lost as the path encounters plantation, swapping the far-reaching panorama for more intimate scenes amongst the rich greens and browns of the forest. Ultimately passing through a gate, you are returned to the head of the track up which the walk began **A**. Follow it back to the main road. ●

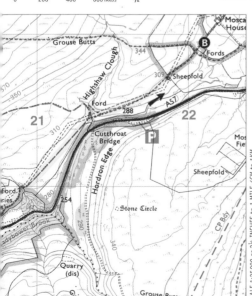

Warslow

		GPS waypoints
Start	Wetton Mill	
Distance	5¼ miles (8.4km)	📍 SK 094 560
Height gain	970 feet (296m)	Ⓐ SK 094 562
Approximate time	2½ hours	Ⓑ SK 091 578
Parking	Car park at start	Ⓒ SK 085 585
Route terrain	Field paths and tracks	Ⓓ SK 086 555
Ordnance Survey maps	Landranger 119 (Buxton & Matlock), Explorer OL24 (The Peak District – White Peak area)	

The popular route through the Manifold Valley follows the railway trail and many people overlook the attractive lane that tags its eastern flank upstream from Wetton Mill. After climbing to Warslow, where there is a village pub, the return is across the undulating countryside above the valley before dropping back alongside Hoo Brook.

📍 Leaving the roadside parking, cross Wetton Mill bridge and go left again beneath the tall cliffs and gaping cave footing Wetton Hill. Entering the yard of Dale Farm, turn left through a gate along a metalled track signed to Hulme End Ⓐ. It undulates pleasantly along the valley below Ecton Hill giving lovely views into the dale.

Farther along, a stream springs from an adit beside the path, betraying the mines that riddle the hill above. They followed rich pipe veins of copper ore, delving almost 1,200 feet (366m) below the level of the river. The deposits were amongst the richest in Britain and generated immense profits for the Duke of Devonshire under whose hand they operated until 1825. He pioneered the use of explosives underground and installed the most efficient pumping engines available at the time to remove flooding water. He even used floating tubs to take the ore out along a sough. A succession of small companies

exploited the workings for another 70 years, but they became increasingly uneconomic and even the arrival of the Manifold Light Railway in 1904 was insufficient to justify their re-opening.

Rounding a bend, Ecton Bridge comes into view and the lane soon ends at a junction. Go over the bridge but then leave immediately through a gap-stile on the right. Cross to a footbridge over Warslow Brook and walk to a wicket gate from which a short path climbs to the trackbed of the old Manifold Light Railway.

Just to the right and before reaching a gate, a path is signed back off left over a stile to Warslow Ⓑ. After a brief indecision, it turns straight up the gorse-covered hillside above the gully of a stream. Beyond a broken wall and then a stile, continue within the edge of a field. Cross another stile by a ruined building and carry on to leave over a stile beside a gate at the top left corner. A trod meanders on across rough

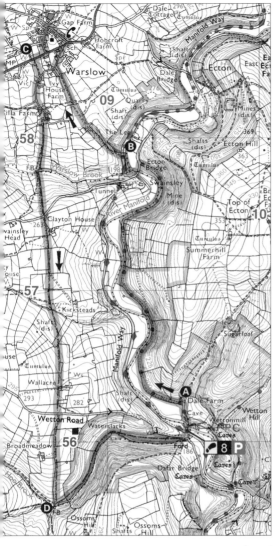

by the left boundary to a second stile and then, with a hedge on your right, walk on to come out onto a lane. Turn right and, at the end, bear right over a cattle-grid along a drive marked to Town End Farm and Barn. Swing right and left to circumvent a garden area, returning to a gate on the right below the cottages.

A contained path leads away to another gate and descend at the field edge to a bridge spanning Warslow Brook. Beyond a patch of scrub, climb away beside a sunken track, dropping into it at some convenient spot higher up to leave through the end gate onto a lane. Carry on along the track's continuation opposite, going forward at a fork. Approaching a cattle-grid, abandon the track in favour of a bridle gate to the right and walk on in the same direction, soon dropping to another stream.

Climb away to a small gate and keep ahead from field to field towards Wallacre Farm. Over its track maintain course, shortly meeting another lane. Walk on into the Hoo Brook valley, now confidently giving up all your height. At the bottom **D**, ignore the bridge and instead go left, accompanying the beckoning stream down the valley. Beyond the crook of the dale, continue along a couple more meadows to meet a lane. Turn right and immediately left back to Wetton Mill. ●

tussock beside a ditched boundary, finally emerging through a small pasture onto a lane. Head right into Warslow.

To find the **Greyhound Inn**, cross the main road, going right and then left up a side street. Otherwise, simply turn left past the church and head west out of the village. About 100 yds past a junction look for a path signed over the left wall below a massive tree **C**. Stay

Lord's Seat

		GPS waypoints
Start	Barber Booth	🥾 SK 107 847
Distance	5½ miles (8.9km)	**A** SK 111 846
Height gain	1,150 feet (351m)	**B** SK 106 840
Approximate time	3 hours	**C** SK 099 829
Parking	Car park west of hamlet beyond railway viaduct	**D** SK 112 834
		E SK 124 834
Route terrain	Moorland paths and tracks, *take care in mist*	**F** SK 124 846
Ordnance Survey maps	Landranger 110 (Sheffield & Huddersfield), Explorer OL1 (The Peak District – Dark Peak area)	

Edale is ringed by high hills, all blessed with superb views. But one of the best vantages is Lord's Seat, which can be attained with only a modest effort. Joining the old road out of the valley to Chapel-en-le-Frith, the route climbs to a shallow saddle and then follows a broad shoulder rising onto the top. Beyond the summit, the path falls along a narrowing grass ridge to Mam Nick then drops from the hill to saunter back across the fields. Alternatively, you can combine this route with that of Walk 15 to continue along the ridge all the way to Lose Hill.

🥾 From the Barber Booth car park, walk back along the lane beneath the railway viaduct. After another 100 yds look for a stile beside a gate on the right **A**. A path heads beside a stream towards Manor House Farm, later slipping across the brook before turning out to a track. Mount a stile opposite, head to the far corner of a paddock and skirt derelict outbuildings to reach the field beyond. Carry on by the boundary to a gate and then strike a diagonal course across more fields to a gate at the top of the intake **B**.

Emerging onto a rough track, turn right through a second gate and fork left to follow Chapel Gate, which rises steadily across the northern flank of the hill. After ½ mile, as you pass a path signed off to Upper Booth and Hayfield,

the gradient levels, the track continuing for a further ¼ mile to a junction of paths in front of a wall **C**. The path left is signed to Castleton and Hope via Mam Tor, and follows the wall for ¾ mile to the top of Lord's Seat **D**.

A raised grass platform to the left of the path is a Bronze Age tumulus, and affords a superb view in every direction. Bounding the opposite side of the Vale of Edale is the steep southern flank of the Kinder plateau, deeply incised by dramatic cloughs that gnaw far back into the hill. To the south lie the limestone hills and dales of the White Peak, prominent among which are the gaunt cliffs of Eldon Hill, which were created by quarrying to produce gravel for road construction.

Although apparently out of the way,

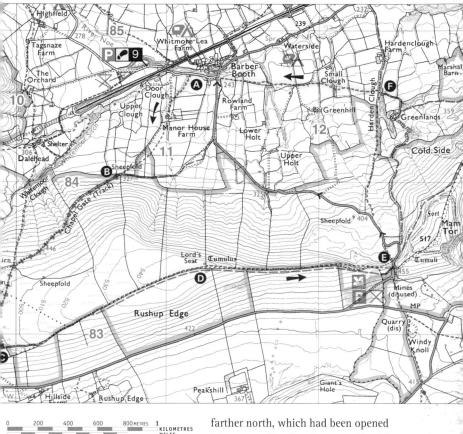

Edale offered a passage between east and west, with packhorse tracks climbing out at the head of the valley to both Chapel-en-le-Frith and Hayfield. It also provided a convenient corridor for a trans-Pennine railway link between Sheffield and Manchester. Work began on the 21-mile line between Dore and Chinley in 1888 and was completed in 1894. The route required two tunnels; Totley, which took the line from Sheffield into the Derwent Valley and another here to break out of the head of Edale. The Cowburn Tunnel, which begins in the cutting below Barber Booth at your feet, is 3,702 yds long and emerges on the western side of the hill above Chapel Milton. The line operated in competition to the Woodhead railway

farther north, which had been opened 50 years earlier. Despite a considerable post-war investment in electrification and new tunnels, Woodhead was eventually closed in 1981. However, this remains a busy commuter line and offers walkers a chance to leave the car at home.

The path runs on beyond the summit, gradually falling more steeply. The ridge progressively narrows before falling abruptly to the lane at Mam Nick **E**. You could, of course, simply return along the lane, but a more pleasant route follows a bridlepath, beginning at a gate by the bus stop, a short way down to the left.

Through the gate branch left and head straight down the hill. Eventually, after curving before a communications mast, the path drops past a large house, Greenlands. Just beyond the house, abandon the path through a gate on the left and follow the drive downhill. Winding through a wooded clough, cross a stream and then immediately climb to a stile on the left **(F)**. Head straight out from field to field, later crossing another deep clough and ultimately emerging at a junction below Barber Booth. The lane opposite, signed to Upper Booth soon returns you to the car park. ●

Looking east from Cown Edge

Pilsbury Castle

		GPS waypoints	
Start	Hartington		SK 128 604
Distance	5½ miles (8.9km)	**Ⓐ**	SK 120 609
Height gain	830 feet (253m)	**Ⓑ**	SK 115 624
Approximate time	2½ hours	**Ⓒ**	SK 115 632
Parking	In village	**Ⓓ**	SK 115 638
Route terrain	Field paths and tracks	**Ⓔ**	SK 124 633
Dog friendly	The bridge across the River Dove leaving Hartington has a metal grid base, which may be a problem for some dogs	**Ⓕ**	SK 130 612
Ordnance Survey maps	Landranger 119 (Buxton & Matlock), Explorer OL24 (The Peak District – White Peak area)		

In contrast to the confines of the lower dales, the hills enclosing upper Dovedale stand back as if to better appreciate the view. This ramble from the old market settlement of Hartington follows their example, contouring the high ground either side of the broad valley to visit the imposing site of an early Norman fortification.

From the centre of Hartington head in the direction of Pilsbury, turning left around the Corner House into Stonewell Lane. Approaching the former cheese factory, leave through a narrow gate on the right, where a field path is signed to Sheen. Beyond a strip of woodland, continue across another field to a stile in the far-left corner. Strike a diagonal to a second stile and maintain course to a footbridge spanning the River Dove. Over it, head for a gate in the top boundary beside a large tree to emerge onto a track **Ⓐ**.

Go right 150 yds to a stile on the left. A sign to Harris Close points an oblique line up a steep, gorse-covered bank. Over a stile at the top, walk within the fringe of a conifer plantation, breaking out to a superb prospect into the higher reaches of the valley. Carry on above the steep slope to a stile and, bearing left, follow a faint trod to another stile

at the field top. Accompany the ongoing wall to the farm at Harris Close, passing left of the buildings, through a yard, and out to a lane.

Walk right to find, after 200 yds, a path signed through a gate on the right **Ⓑ**. Take the stile immediately on the left, crossing a small rough paddock and then turn left along a short contained path to a stile behind a cottage. A slanting trod ushers you back towards the dale, making for the distant mounds of Pilsbury Castle seen on the opposite flank. Passing from the second field, the path briefly hugs a wall above the head of a marshy fold before resuming its downward trend. Meeting a walled track shaded by tall pine, head down to a footbridge and ford below Pilsbury **Ⓒ**.

Observant eyes will notice that the track's containing walls are of different materials, limestone on the left and sandstone to the right. The river here flows in the margin between the two types of rock, their diverse characters determining the vegetation and thus reflected in the general appearance of the opposing hillsides.

Over the river, the track climbs to a lane below Pilsbury Farm. Go left to a hairpin bend, and keep forward through a gate along another track. It continues up the valley to Pilsbury Castle, which is accessed through a gate at the end **D**.

Despite the lack of stout curtain walls, high embattled towers and turreted keep, Pilsbury Castle presents a powerful image of formidable defence. It was built around the end of the 10th century by Henri de Ferrières, one of the French nobles who joined William's invasion of England in 1066. The earthen banks and ditches exploit the lie of the land and an outcrop of imposing limestone reef, their effectiveness originally heightened by wooden palisades along the top. Strategically overlooking the river, the fortification would have controlled the

ford as well as passage up and down the valley and was probably built as a deterrent to further opposition following the failed northern rebellion. But as internal peace settled, it became redundant, being remote from the kingdom's borders.

After exploring the site, leave by the same gate and bear right on a rising path above the track along which you arrived. Reaching the crest, glance back to appreciate the castle's location and effectiveness as guardian of the valley and continue through a gap. The path levels above Pilsbury Farm, eventually swinging left across a final field to a narrow lane. Over a stile opposite, bear left to a wall gap and follow a trod along a broad, grassy fold, passing a gnarled marker stone to reach a distant wall **E**.

Ignoring the stile, climb right to a small gate in the top corner. Head away, skirting a couple of corners before dropping to a gateway by a pair of tall trees. A distinct trod meanders across a

Above Bridge End Farm looking back to Beresford Dale

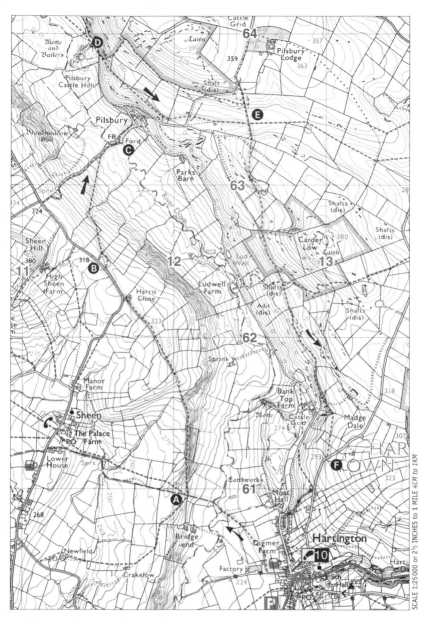

succession of upland enclosures, passing through an access area below Carder Low and then crossing a line of bell pit mines that followed a vein of lead ore across the hill. Eventually, the way runs above Bank Top Farm to meet the bend of a concrete track. Take the uphill branch, abandoning it as you pass into the higher field to stay with the right-hand wall to a stile. Continue across more fields, emerging over a final stile beyond a barn onto a lane **F**.

Walk down the hill, shortly turning off, just before a cream-painted cottage, onto a descending walled track. Coming out onto a lower lane, follow it left back into Hartington. ●

SCALE 1:25000 or 2½ INCHES to 1 MILE 4CM to 1KM

Win Hill and Thornhill

		GPS waypoints	
Start	Ashopton	🥾	SK 202 858
Distance	6¼ miles (10.1km)	Ⓐ	SK 197 855
Height gain	1,350 feet (411m)	Ⓑ	SK 201 830
Approximate time	3 hours	Ⓒ	SK 197 837
Parking	Heatherdene car park, off A6013	Ⓓ	SK 191 850
Route terrain	Tracks and forest paths	Ⓔ	SK 186 850
		Ⓕ	SK 182 850
Ordnance Survey maps	Landranger 110 (Sheffield & Huddersfield), Explorer OL1 (The Peak District – Dark Peak area)	Ⓖ	SK 190 860

Although not the highest, its position overlooking the confluence of three valleys gives Win Hill Pike one of the finest prospects in the Derwent Valley. It is approached here on a roundabout route from Heatherdene above the Ladybower Dam adopting the course of a former railway to Thornhill. The steady ascent to the summit is by way of the hill's southern spur, heightening the anticipation for the view from the top. The more direct descent follows woodland paths back to the lake.

🥾 A sign beside the **toilets** indicates a path to the dam. Drop to the road and cross the dam to the other side of the valley Ⓐ. Turning left, take the descending track signed to Thornhill. After 250 yds, watch for the Touchstone Trail branching right along an old railway trackbed. A narrow-gauge line,

The Ladybower viaduct

it was built to carry construction materials to the Howden and Derwent dams. Contouring the steep valley, it later breaks out to more open country-side, revealing a superb view to Bamford Edge. Below is the village of Bamford, its steepled church rising above the buildings. It was there that the dead of Ashopton graveyard were re-interred before the village was flooded beneath the Ladybower Reservoir.

Reaching a lane, cross and continue along the track for another good ½ mile. At a cottage Ⓑ, just before the trail's end, turn off sharp right through a gate and climb back above the track, to meet a lane at the foot of Thornhill. Walk up into the village, keeping right at a junction by a red telephone box. As the lane then bends, bear left on a track beside a cottage. Reaching a second cottage, go right, meandering down past it to the Thornhill Town Well.

Although not a well in the traditional sense, it supplied the village until piped water finally arrived in 1949, despite the dams in the upper valley having been built 30 years previously. Water seeps from the hill where porous sandstone meets impervious shale and is collected for cattle in a trough, compartmentalised for cleaning. Drinking water for the villagers was collected higher up away from the animals.

Turn back towards the cottage, but then go sharp right to climb above the well. Through a gate, carry on across the steep hillside. Reaching a fork, branch left at a sign to Win Hill, rising to a track beside another cottage **C**.

To the right, a narrow way hedged with old holly bushes makes a steady ascent of the hill. Through a gate higher up, carry on between gorse scrub and, ignoring a crossing path down to Yorkshire Bridge, ultimately reach a kissing-gate onto the open heath. Climb

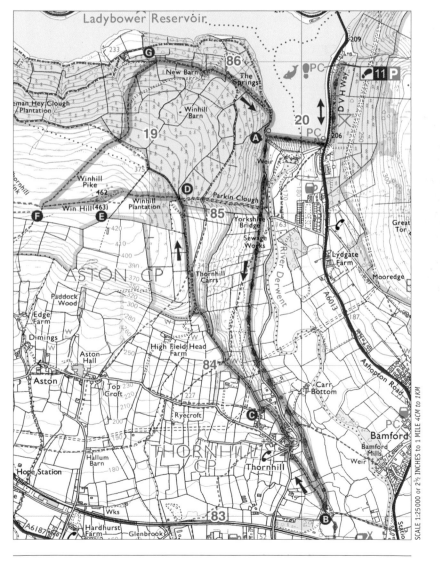

SCALE 1:25000 or 2½ INCHES to 1 MILE 4CM to 1KM

Across the Ashop Valley to Crook Hill

left beside the wall to a higher path and go right, a lesser gradient allowing a more leisurely appreciation of the scene opening along the Derwent Valley. Joining a path from Aston, keep ahead towards a forest plantation, staying right at a fork to reach a four-way signpost **D**. Turn left, rising at the fringe of trees and then up a bare hillside for the final assault on the top **E**.

Despite the glorious views that have accompanied virtually the whole ascent, there is still a climax awaiting you at the summit. To the west lies the Mam Tor Ridge with Kinder Scout behind and to the east, Bamford Edge rimming an expanse of moor that stretches back to Sheffield. The flooded upper reaches of the Derwent Valley wind between the folds of its flanking hills, rising to a distant watershed with Longdendale. Limestone country lies to the south of Castleton, although that is bracketed by the outrunning tongues of the gritstone cap.

Continue past the summit, dropping to join a broader path beside the fence. Walk for $\frac{1}{4}$ mile until you reach the second of two gates, where a battered signpost marks a junction of paths **F**. Turning sharp right, strike across a sea of heather below the northern flank of Win Hill towards the edge of the forest. Signed through a gate, a path drops among the trees, areas of which have been cleared and replanted, opening, for the time being at least, a last view across the valley.

Ignore a crossing track encountered lower down, descending to another track **G**. Follow this to the right, soon reaching a junction. Keep ahead to the next junction and turn right. However, almost immediately, branch off left through a small gate and carry on down the wooded hillside to come out onto a broad track by the lakeside. Go right to the foot of the reservoir and retrace your outward steps across the dam back to the car park. ●

Chee Dale

Start	Miller's Dale	GPS waypoints	
Distance	5¾ miles (9.3km)	🥾	SK 138 732
Height gain	1,290 feet (393m)	**Ⓐ**	SK 130 733
Approximate time	3 hours	**Ⓑ**	SK 127 734
		Ⓒ	SK 112 726
Parking	Car park at former station (Pay and Display)	**Ⓓ**	SK 123 720
		Ⓔ	SK 133 717
Route terrain	Field and woodland paths, the one through Chee Dale being rocky, requiring occasional clambering and briefly along stepping stones that can be flooded during spate	**Ⓕ**	SK 133 731
Ordnance Survey maps	Landranger 119 (Buxton & Matlock), Explorer OL24 (The Peak District – White Peak area)		

The River Wye's passage through the limestone gorges of the Peak is forever twisting, but nowhere is it more contorted than in the short, dramatic section above Miller's Dale known as Chee Dale. This secluded chasm is particularly beautiful and so constricted that, at one point, the river completely fills the narrow ravine and the path resorts to stepping stones. The walk returns across the upland fields and an old trackway ignored by the modern road network. The path through Chee Dale is occasionally flooded, but Walk 6 through Monk's Dale, also beginning along the Monsal Trail, offers an alternative ramble for the day.

🥾 Leaving the car park, walk past the old platforms of Miller's Dale Station and follow the track right, signed as the Monsal Trail to Chee Dale and Buxton. Beyond the East Buxton Lime Kilns, a high viaduct carries the former railway across the River Wye to the portal of a tunnel burrowing beneath Chee Tor, but through which there is now no passage. Instead, leave the trail immediately after the viaduct. Go through a couple of gates on the right **Ⓐ** and follow a descending trod, again signed to Chee Dale, across a hillside meadow to a footbridge over the river.

On the opposite bank **Ⓑ**, scale a stile on the left and head upriver until the path veers above the gushing eruptions of Wormhill Springs. After crossing a footbridge at the foot of Flag Dale, the path resumes its course up Chee Dale, clambering over rocks and then passing beneath towering, overhung cliffs dripping water. Higher up, the gorge narrows further and the path is forced into the riverbed along a string of sturdy stepping stones. *Should the river be in spate and the stepping stones impassable, you can rescue the day by going back to Point* **Ⓑ** *and following*

The railway enters the narrow gorge of Chee Dale

Walk 6 through Wormhill and Monk's Dale instead.

Returning to dry ground around the bend, go over a footbridge below a lofty viaduct and carry on at a higher level above the river. After a short distance, double back at a Monsal Trail sign to Blackwell Mill, climbing to the disused railway as it emerges from beneath Chee Tor. Walk across the viaduct and through a short tunnel to continue high above the river. Despite the elevation and superb prospect into the gorge, the position remains dwarfed by the soaring cliffs containing the deep rift.

Over 300 feet (91m) deep and, at one point, completely taken up by the river, Chee Dale is one of the most spectacular sections of the River Wye's valley. Bound by high, overhanging limestone cliffs, it presented a considerable challenge to the engineers of the London Midland Railway as they forced their line towards Manchester. The railway from Derby reached Buxton in 1863 and was continued north via Great Rocks Dale when the Dove Holes Tunnel opened a couple of years later. As well as carrying considerable passenger

traffic, the line enabled vast quarries to be developed within the gorge. The stone was burnt in massive kilns built beside the track to produce quicklime, a substance demanded in huge quantities by the building, chemical and smelting industries as well as for use as an agricultural fertiliser. The East Buxton Lime Kilns, which you earlier passed, opened in 1880 and were in operation until 1944.

Beyond another short tunnel the trail again swaps banks and soon forks at a junction that took the line through Great Rocks Dale via Chinley to Manchester. However, stick with the left branch along Wye Dale, which led to Buxton, in a little while passing beneath a bridge **Ⓒ**. Over a stile on the left, climb to the track above and follow it from the bridge up a narrow side valley.

Part-way up, a path is signed to Blackwell over a stile on the left. Zigzagging steeply, it pauses at a promontory overlooking Wye Dale, from which there is a magnificent view. Leaving the prospect, continue up the hill to then level beside a wall. Over a stile keep going in the adjacent field, but in the next field, veer to a gate in the distant corner. Stay by the right wall to a second gate, joining a track up to

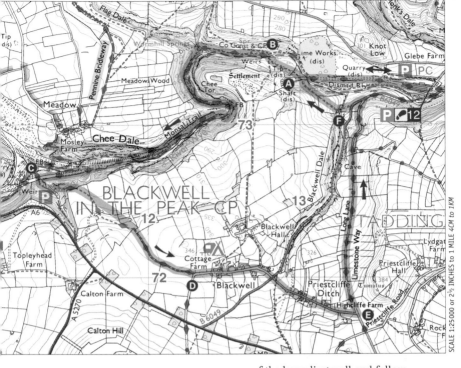

SCALE 1:25000 or 2½ INCHES to 1 MILE 4CM to 1KM

meet the Pennine Bridleway. Follow it left through a gate and on across the fields to meet the corner of a lane **D**.

Walk ahead past the scattered dwellings of Blackwell, continuing over a crossroads towards Priestcliffe and Taddington. Where the rising lane eventually bends sharp right, abandon it for a broad, walled track on the left, the Limestone Way **E**. Aptly named Long Lane, the track steadily loses height for the next $^3/_4$ mile, revealing a superb view into Wye Dale and the foot of Monk's Dale. It eventually leads to the B6049, just west of Miller's Dale.

Go left to the bend, leaving there over a stile on the right **F**. Drop left, across a sloping meadow to a stream emanating from Blackwell Dale and cross to a stile on the opposite bank. Climb steeply to the top-right corner of the meadow. Pass through the broken corner of the bounding wall and follow a path falling between the trees into the valley. It ends over a stile onto the Monsal Trail at Point **A**. Go back over the viaduct to the Miller's Dale car park.

●

The stepping stones in Chee Dale

Standedge Tunnel

Start	Marsden, by the station	**GPS waypoints**	
Distance	6 miles (9.7km)	🗺 SE 047 118	
Height gain	950 feet (290m)	Ⓐ SE 039 119	
Approximate time	3 hours	Ⓑ SE 005 079	
Parking	Car park by Marsden Station	Ⓒ SE 014 086	
Route terrain	Rough tracks	Ⓓ SE 018 094	
Ordnance Survey maps	Landranger 110 (Sheffield & Huddersfield), Explorers OL21 (South Pennines) and OL1 (The Peak District – Dark Peak area)	Ⓔ SE 031 100	
		Ⓕ SE 032 119	

The sprawling Pennine hills might seem an insurmountable obstacle to waterborne traffic, yet the heyday of the Industrial Revolution saw three separate canals pushed across the watershed. The Huddersfield Narrow Canal was the boldest of these ventures, topping out at 643 feet (196m) above sea-level in a 5,500-yard (5,029m) long tunnel that burrows 636 feet (194m) below the moorland summit. Now re-opened after years of dereliction, you can enjoy the unique experience of a three-hour boat journey though the tunnel as preface to this superb return over the hill following the old route taken by the draw-horses.
Pre-booked trips currently operate (2009) on the first Saturday of the month between Easter and October. For information call 01484 844298 or email info@standedge.co.uk.

The crucial section of the Huddersfield Narrow Canal lay in the Standedge Tunnel, but was beset with problems almost from the beginning. The Diggle end had to be restarted after a survey found it several feet higher than the Marsden portal and incorrect alignment of individual sections, dug from a line of airshafts across the moor, left a wavering course. Flooding and collapse delayed its completion by 12 years and, desperate for revenue, the owners resorted to packhorses to transport goods over the moors until the

connection was made.

When the tunnel finally opened, traffic was brisk, but with only occasional passing places, boats had to take their turn going through. As 'time was money', fights often broke out between crews reluctant to give way and, in the end, an alternate one-way operation had to be imposed with official 'leggers' walking boats through at a shilling a trip. The competitive spirit, however, remained and David Whitehead set an incredible record of 1 hour 25 minutes in 1914. Commercial

Boarding the boat to pass through the longest, highest and deepest canal tunnel in Britain

traffic ended in 1921 and the tunnel was finally closed in 1944, but following its restoration in 2001, Whitehead's daughter Lilly Turner was invited to re-open the tunnel.

✎ Leaving the car park, turn right and, following a sign for the Standedge Tunnel, join the towpath of the Huddersfield Narrow Canal. Continue for ½ mile before crossing a footbridge over the canal. To the right, there is a small exhibition in a former warehouse detailing the history of the tunnel and its restoration, while to the left is the Marsden portal of the tunnel **Ⓐ**, where a **café** offers refreshment while you wait for your boat.

Today's electrically powered craft do nothing to diminish the feeling of awe on entering the tunnel and it is not hard to imagine the forbidding prospect facing the boatmen of a century ago who legged their heavily laden boats through the long, dank passage. A flickering candle might have been all the light they had until they finally emerged into Lancashire from the Diggle portal.

Disembarking **Ⓑ**, follow the towpath back past the tunnel entrance and through a small car park onto the street. Go right and swing right again over the railway bridge, turning left at the other side past the **Diggle Hotel**, a convenient stop for refreshment. Signed as the Pennine Bridleway to Standedge, the rising way degrades to a track that gives a fine view into the head of the valley above the town.

Later passing a house, the track becomes metalled, but as it then bends left, leave through a small gate ahead **Ⓒ** onto a rough track. Still signed the Pennine Bridleway, it continues up the hillside. Higher up, by one of the ventilation shafts marking the line of the tunnel, the track swings left past an abandoned homestead. At a three-way fingerpost, take the right branch and, through a gate walk past the small Brun Clough Reservoir to a car park beside the A62 **Ⓓ**.

The Pennine Way leaves beside the entrance, rising above the deep cutting of the main road, excavated in 1839 to carry the Wakefield and Austerlands Toll Road. Passing through a gate onto the National Trust Marsden Moor Estate, the path curves above Redbrook Reservoir. Approaching an old stone boundary post, ignore the path off right and instead dip left across a stream to resume the ongoing track. After some ¾ mile it eventually narrows and drops to ford a stream at the head of Carr Clough. Climb out onto a narrow lane.

Walk left for just over ¼ mile. As the lane descends, look for a path on the

Tunnel End Cottages at Marsden

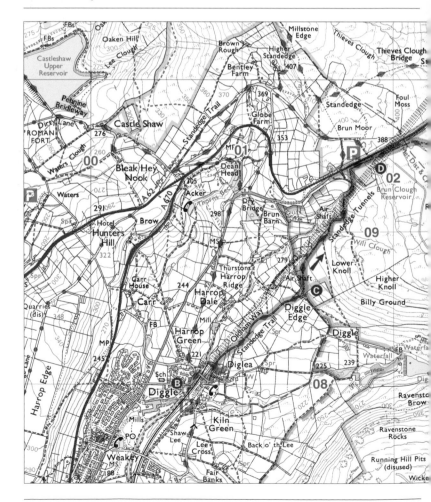

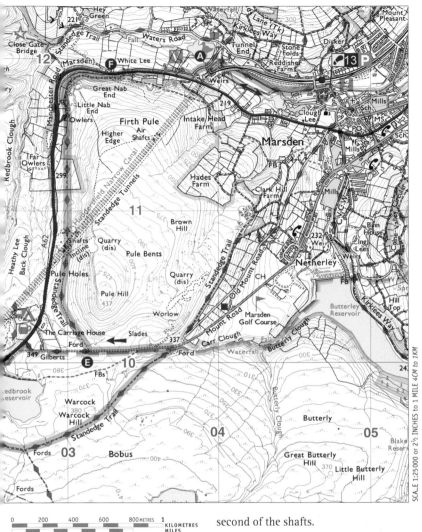

0	200	400	600	800 METRES	1
					KILOMETRES
					MILES
0	200	400	600 YARDS		½

right marked as the Standedge Trail **E**. It contours the western flank of Pule Hill, whose upper slopes have been quarried to a rugged profile of broken cliffs. The path soon turns above the main road and affords a spectacular view across a moorland amphitheatre, draining to the head of the River Colne. Approaching more ventilation shafts, pass above the first and cross a path to the quarries above. Keep ahead on the trod following the line of an overhead power cable and passing below the

second of the shafts.

Beyond a couple of intervening stiles, join a wall on your left to pass behind two houses. After the wall later ends, the path falls to meet the road over a stile **F**. Cross and go right, branching off after 300 yds down a cul de sac drive. Where that bends, bear right onto a walled grass track. At a junction beyond a house, go left and then, immediately over a bridge, turn through a gap on the right. Follow the path left, descending a grass bank to return to the canal by the Marsden end of the tunnel. Retrace your outward steps along the towpath to the car park. ●

Broomhead Reservoir

		GPS waypoints	
Start	Bolsterstone	🖉	SK 270 967
Distance	6 miles (9.7km)	**A**	SK 269 963
Height gain	1,000 feet (305m)	**B**	SK 272 958
Approximate time	3 hours	**C**	SK 255 959
Parking	By village church	**D**	SK 248 957
Route terrain	Woodland and field paths and good tracks	**E**	SK 241 962
		F	SK 241 969
Ordnance Survey maps	Landranger 110 (Sheffield & Huddersfield), Explorer OL1 (The Peak District – Dark Peak area)		

The adjacent valleys of the Little Don and Ewden could hardly be more different, the one home to what was once one of the largest steel works in England while in the other, forest drapes the valley side above a couple of lakes. From the tiny village of Bolsterstone, the route is one of downs and ups, first dropping beside the Broomhead Reservoir, climbing to the parkland of Broomhead Hall and then descending to cross the valley at Ewden Bridge. A final climb through woodland and grazing returns the walk along the broad ridge dividing the two valleys, an enjoyable stroll heightened by extensive views.

The tiny village of Bolsterstone traces its origins to Saxon times and stood on an ancient packhorse trail along which salt was brought from Cheshire. The substantial bolster stones themselves are to be found in the churchyard, removed there for safekeeping from the village green in the 19th century. Their origin is obscure, although it has been suggested they might have been the base of either a gibbet or a double cross. Other relics in the village include the stocks by the lychgate and an old water pump and trough beside the village hall, which was formerly the National School and built in 1852.

🖉 Head south out of the village past the village hall. At a junction, bear right and go steeply downhill, keeping right again at a second fork lower down. After

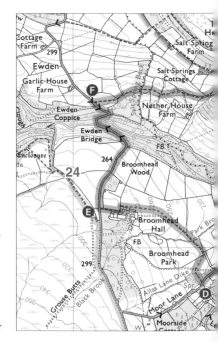

200 yds, look for a path signed off on the left **A**, which drops through a wood. Crossing a stream, turn left and follow its bank to a small service reservoir, from where a broader path falls to meet a track by a wood-boarded cottage. Follow that left past houses to reach a lane. Carry on downhill to a junction, taking the lane opposite and crossing the outflow from the Broomhead Reservoir.

Leave on the bend beyond, where a footpath is signed into Horse Wood **B**. It rises gently through the trees, passing the dam to continue above the Broomhead Reservoir. Eventually the path meets a lane, but you can avoid the tarmac by hugging the wooded shore. After $^1/_2$ mile, a wooden walkway takes the path across a stream, Lee Lane Dike. At the end of the planking, leave through a gap in the fence **C** and cross to a broad track opposite. Climb through the forest to emerge on Allas Lane and carry on up the hill. After passing a gateway into Broomhead Park, and before reaching a road

St Mary's Church and the Bolsterstones

junction, leave over a waymarked wall stile on the right **D**.

Bear right from the wall across a couple of streams, beyond which a waymark directs you towards a gate where fence and wall meet. Continuing

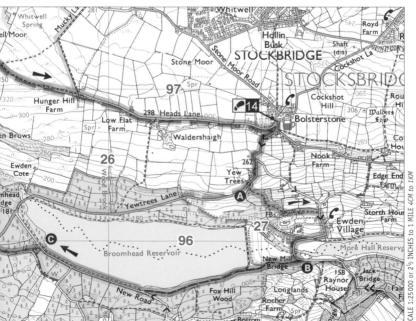

through more gates, follow a fence up the slope towards Broomhead Hall, which soon comes into view. The way remains in the field, bypassing farm cottages to a wall stile in the corner. A path ushers you to a track, which in turn, leads out to a lane **E**.

Head steeply downhill to cross Ewden Bridge and climb the equally severe gradient beyond. After walking 150 yds beyond a sharp left-hand bend, look for a footpath signed off through a field-gate on the right **F**. Bear right across the field, taking the prominent rounded hill on the skyline above as your mark. Through a gate keep going between the trees and across a stream. Stay above a bracken bank, picking up an obvious path through a belt of wood. Ignore a crossing path higher up and continue over a stile. The way angles ever-upwards through bracken and gorse scrub, making for the top corner of another plantation.

There, the path turns up beside a wall, passing through a gateway to join a rough track from Salt Springs Cottage and Farm. Follow it over the crest of the hill, where it then turns alongside the edge of Whitwell Moor. Gently

Beside the Broomhead Reservoir

descending for $1\frac{1}{2}$ miles along the spine of a broad ridge, from which there are views over the valley and across to neighbouring Stocksbridge, it eventually leads back to Bolsterstone.

The town of Stocksbridge lies just to the north, overlooking the massive steel works that run along the base of the valley for much of its length. Before Samuel Fox arrived in 1842 looking for a suitable place to set up a wire drawing mill, the settlement had a population of only 34. Fox began his business in an abandoned corn mill, producing wire for the manufacture of pins and later for his 'Paragon' folding umbrella frame, which he invented in 1851. His firm went on to develop a range of specialised products, which included railway lines, springs for Rolls Royce and, later, steels for the aviation industry. Such was the scale of business, that in 1872 a branch line was brought into the valley to service the mills, which, at their peak, employed over 7,000 people. The works are now owned by Corus, part of the Indian steel giant, Tata, and, despite a downturn in the industry and clouds of threatened closure, plans have now been put forward for investment to produce hi-tech steels for the aerospace industry. ●

Lose Hill

Start	Edale		GPS waypoints
Distance	6 miles (9.7km)		🖊 SK 123 853
Height gain	1,650 feet (503m)		Ⓐ SK 123 852
Approximate time	3½ hours		Ⓑ SK 125 833
Parking	Car park below village – Pay and Display		Ⓒ SK 136 845
			Ⓓ SK 153 853
Route terrain	Generally good upland paths		Ⓔ SK 143 848
Ordnance Survey maps	Landranger 110 (Sheffield & Huddersfield), Explorer OL1 (The Peak District – Dark Peak area)		

The long ridge of high ground separating the Vale of Edale from Castleton nestling at the head of the Hope Valley is one of the classic walks of the Peak District and provides stunning views almost every step of the way. It is here begun from the village of Edale and can be combined with Walk 9 over Lord's Seat to create a challenging exploration of the complete ridge.

🖊 From the Edale car park, follow the main lane to the right. Just beyond the de-restriction sign, a track Ⓐ to Hardenclough Farm and signed as a footpath to Castleton takes you across the River Noe. As the ground rises the eye is drawn towards the steep northern flank of Mam Tor, and the full line of the day's walk can be traced along the ridge to Lose Hill. The scene is equally absorbing to the right, where a great amphitheatre of high ground defines the head of the Edale Valley.

Beyond Hardenclough Farm, the track swings across a boisterous stream and rises energetically to the next farm, Greenlands. Just before its private entrance, leave through a bridle gate on the left. Take the path to the right, which is signed Mam Tor and gains height across the steep flank of the hill. A final pull leads to the high pass of Mam Nick, joining the lane for the last few yards to the top. Through a gate on

the left Ⓑ, a good path doubles back onto the summit of Mam Tor. Along the way are set reminders of the people who constructed the prehistoric fort on its top; a piece of pottery, an iron torque, a plough and depictions of dwellings.

On a clear day, the panorama from the top is superb; Kinder and the flat-topped, high moorland of the Dark Peak lie to the north, while along the valley beyond Castleton lies a very different landscape of grassy limestone hills. Particularly striking are Winnats Pass and Cave Dale, deep gorges cutting back into the steep slope of the main valley behind the town.

Mam Tor's commanding position above two adjacent valleys proclaimed status for the Bronze Age people who came here to bury their tribal leaders some 3,500 years ago. Some time later, a village grew around the ceremonial site and the flattened platforms of around 100 dwellings and store huts

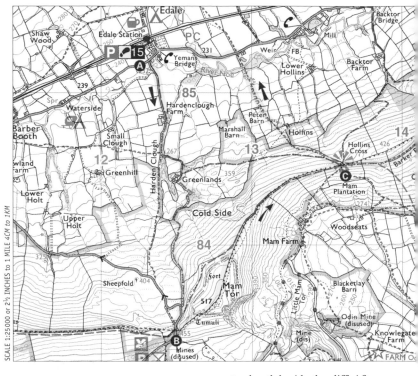

```
0    200   400   600   800 METRES   1
                                    KILOMETRES
                                    MILES
0    200   400   600 YARDS   ½
```

dotted around the summit can still be seen. The most impressive man-made feature is the ditch and rampart defence of an Iron Age hill fort, which would, in its day, have been even more imposing, topped with a high wooden palisade and later a stone wall. Much, however, is still to be learned about this intriguing site, which is the second highest known hill fort in Britain.

After the strenuous ascent from Edale, the next leg of the route appears positively inviting. Beginning with an attenuated, gradual fall to the shallow saddle of Hollins Cross **C**, it continues over Back Tor to Lose Hill at the far end of the long ridge, still some 2 miles distant. The path sticks to the top of the narrow spine almost all the way and affords a splendid view on either side. Approaching the foot of the craggy northern face of Back Tor, the way slips over a stile on the left and clambers up

a good path beside the cliff. After admiring the view from the top of the rocky precipice, and perhaps adding to the efforts of the pebble artists on the nearby cairn, continue along the final stretch to Lose Hill **D**.

There is nothing remarkable about the top of the hill except, of course, the view, which is celebrated in a topograph naming seemingly just about everything for miles around. Prominent across the mouth of the Noe Valley is Win Hill, its summit cone looking something of an afterthought to finish off the job. Since the middle of the 20th century, Lose Hill has acquired another name, Ward's Piece, bestowed to honour G. H. B. Ward. Among many other causes he was a leading activist in the fight for public access to the moors during the early 20th century. Ward founded the Sheffield Clarion Ramblers in 1900, the first club of its type for working class people and was involved with several other footpath societies, as well as the Ramblers' Association and

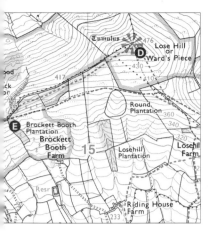

took with it the main road out of Castleton to the west.

Returning to the stile at the foot of Back Tor , *you then have a choice of routes. Immediately before the stile, a path descends fairly steeply off the hill. Lower down, it joins a track through the intake wall, which leads past Backtor Farm out to the lane. Alternatively, you may wish to hang on to your hard-won height for a little longer, in which case, stick with the ridge path until you reach Hollins Cross* ●. Bear right there and then take the lower branch where it shortly splits, the path heading towards Grindslow Knoll, the prominent hill above Edale on the opposite side of the valley. Through a gate at the bottom, drop to a track from Hollins Farm, which also takes you to the lane. Edale and the car park lie to the left.

the Youth Hostel Association. It was the Ramblers' Association who bought Lose Hill for him in 1945, which he then generously presented to the National Trust.

Although surrounded by access land on its upper slopes, there is no way off the hill into the Edale Valley. You can drop off south to either Hope or Castleton, both quite acceptable routes, but it is then a long walk back to Edale. The sensible choice is to retrace your steps along the ridge, where you will find the views revealed in a completely new light. Particularly impressive is the massive ongoing slump on the eastern face of Mam Tor, that in 1979 finally

Hollins Cross stands on a high pass at a junction of ancient paths, one of which was a medieval coffin route along which mourners from Edale carried their dead across the hill for burial at the parish church in Castleton. With the arrival of the industrial age, the direction of passage across the hill was reversed as people from Castleton trudged across to work in Edale's textile mill. ●

Hollins Cross and Mam Tor

Lyme Park and the Macclesfield Canal

		GPS waypoints
Start	Nelson Pit, Higher Poynton	🖋 SJ 944 833
Distance	6¼ miles (10.1km)	Ⓐ SJ 945 820
Height gain	625 feet (191m)	Ⓑ SJ 948 814
Approximate time	3 hours	Ⓒ SJ 962 824
Parking	Car park at start	Ⓓ SJ 961 827
Route terrain	Tracks and clear paths across fields and parkland	Ⓔ SJ 963 841
		Ⓕ SJ 951 843
Dog friendly	Dogs should be kept on leads within deer park	
Ordnance Survey maps	Landranger 109 (Manchester), Explorer OL1 (The Peak District – Dark Peak area)	

The Lyme Park estate cascades from the sparse moors to the rich farmland of the Cheshire plain, where the Macclesfield Canal picks a meandering course at the foot of the hills. This pleasant amble wanders between the two, swapping far-reaching vistas for more intimate countryside scenes.

Nelson Pit was one of more than 70 sunk around Higher Poyton during the 19th century, exploiting a coal seam some 400 feet (122m) below the surface. Although 30–40 men only worked many, collectively they were a significant local employer until the last mine closed in 1935. Several of the former pit heads are still identifiable beside the canal as hollows and mounds of spoil. Now overgrown with bramble and birch trees they have become havens for wildlife.

🖋 From the visitor centre, where you can glean something of the area's history, follow the drive to the upper parking area beside the Macclesfield Canal. Head right along the towpath, crossing a footbridge at Mount Vernon Wharf, where coal from the Nelson Pit was loaded onto waiting narrowboats. Beyond a road bridge, the canal

broadens to a pool, the result of mining subsidence. Farther on, beside a metal footbridge, notice a circular stone base that once supported a swivel bridge.

The railway age had already arrived when the Macclesfield Canal was opened in 1831, and it was one of the country's last major waterways. Linking the Peak Forest and Trent and Mersey canals, the 'Macc' was nevertheless profitable and, as well as coal, carried silk and cotton to the mills and gritstone from quarries in the Pennine foothills. Despite the adjacent railway opening in 1869, commercial traffic continued into the 1950s. By that time the canal had already become a popular recreational waterway, being adopted as the home water of the country's first canal users club, the North Cheshire Cruising Club, which was formed in 1943.

After another ¼ mile, the canal

swings right, carried on a high aqueduct above the valley. Approaching a bridge (number 17), leave the towpath for the track above **A**.

Over the canal, the track passes a cluster of cottages, narrowing beyond a gate to enter a field. Carry on alongside the right-hand hedge until, partway along the second field a sign indicates a concessionary path branching left to Redacre Cottage. Exiting the field by the cottage, go right past the buildings of

Redacre Farm and then swing left to leave along a track to Shrigley Road. To the left, the lane falls to a shallow bend in front of Green Close Methodist Church **B**.

Immediately past the church, abandon the lane, bearing right along a track that drops to a bridge beside West Parkgate Lodge. Continue along the

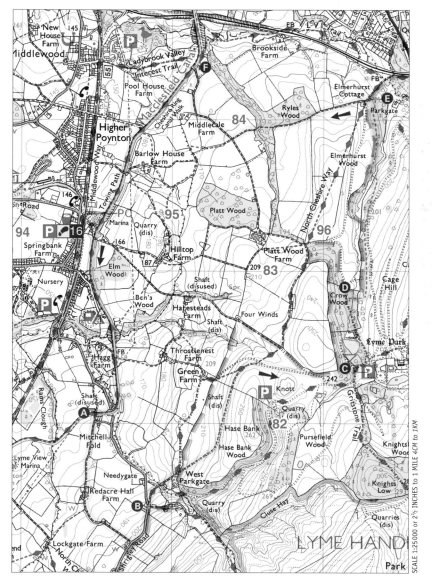

SCALE 1:25000 or 2½ INCHES to 1 MILE 4CM to 1KM

Winter sunset on the Macclesfield Canal

track to a fork and keep ahead, mounting a ladder-stile beside a gate to follow a field track across rough pasture around the flank of Hase Bank. It later passes through a gate onto the National Trust estate.

The way shortly curves right, opening a view, firstly of the Cage, an ornate 16th-century hunting tower, and then a folly tower, high on the hillside in Lantern Wood. Carry on as tracks join from either side and then bear left, following a tarmac drive towards the main parking area below the hall. Keep left past the car park to a junction in front of the information centre **C**.

To visit the gardens and house, where there is a **restaurant**, take the stepped path beside the information centre. Otherwise, turn left along the drive overlooking the millpond. Approaching the stables and timber yard (where there is a **coffee shop**), bear right bypassing a small service area to a gate into the woodland behind. Follow the path for 100 yds to a fork by a stream that emanates from the lake **D**.

Take the right branch beside the stream to reach a ladder-stile at the far end of the wood. Rising away, the path swings left along the valley at a higher level. After briefly paralleling the drive, the path drops over a stile into Elmerhurst Wood. Crossing the stream, walk above the opposite bank, eventually leaving the trees onto a farm track **E**.

Heading left, it leads over a cattle-grid to a junction in front of Elmerhurst Cottage. Bear off beside it, following a sign pointing to Middle Wood into the field behind and continue with the boundary. At the far side of the second field, drop through trees to a bridge spanning a stream. Climb to the field above and stay with the left hedge. Passing out onto another farm track, turn right. On reaching a junction by Middlecale Farm, go right again, shortly crossing a bridge over the canal by a wartime pillbox **F**.

Joining the towpath on the opposite bank, double back beneath the bridge. The final $^{3}/_{4}$ mile passes several of the abandoned pits before returning you to the marina and car park. ●

Beeley and Hob Hurst's House

Beeley and Hob Hurst's House

		GPS waypoints	
Start	Beeley		SK 265 674
Distance	6¼ miles (10.1km)	**A**	SK 265 676
Height gain	950 feet (290m)	**B**	SK 270 684
Approximate time	3 hours	**C**	SK 271 690
Parking	Considerate roadside parking in the village	**D**	SK 278 685
		E	SK 287 692
Route terrain	Good tracks and clear field paths	**F**	SK 282 687
		G	SK 279 675
Ordnance Survey maps	Landranger 119 (Buxton & Matlock), Explorer OL24 (The Peak District – White Peak area)	**H**	SK 269 666

The high moors were not always as deserted as they appear today, once supporting communities of farmers who have left their mark in traces of field systems and innumerable burial mounds. One of the most unusual is known as Hob Hurst's House and is visited on this walk from the pretty estate village of Beeley. The route contrasts open hillside with thick woodland plantation and offers outstanding views across the Derwent Valley.

Although close to Chatsworth, Beeley retained its independence until the third Duke began acquiring the neighbouring

Climbing onto Beeley Moor

land to extend his estate. Over time, cottages, a reading room, school and new chapel were put up for the benefit of the estate workers and the Norman church dedicated to St Anne was largely

rebuilt, although vestiges of the original work survive around the doorway and in carved heads gazing down from the walls. The **village inn,** which has earned a reputation for its food, dates from the 17th century, when in addition to farming, coal mining and stone quarrying were important industries, while just south of the village the stream cascading down the hillside powered a lead smelting mill.

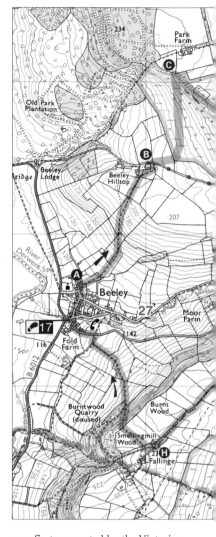

📷 Take the street opposite the **Devonshire Arms**, climbing through the village beside the **Old Smithy café**. Keep left at a triangular green, passing the entrance to the church car park. Just beyond, look for a squeeze stile set back on the right behind New House Ⓐ. Head away, along a narrow pasture, continuing in a second field to the distant top-left corner. A slanting trod carries on to the brow of the hill, over which the way follows a wall to Beeley Hilltop. Walk past the farmhouse and keep right in front of cow sheds before turning left through a yard to emerge onto a track Ⓑ.

A few yards to the right, go over a stile on the left. Bear right to a second stile onto the open moor. A clear path left strikes an oblique ascent across a steep, bracken-clad hillside, broaching the top to meet a broad track Ⓒ.

Take time to admire the view back across the valley before following the track gently uphill to the right. Approaching the crest, look for a waymarked path leaving on the left Ⓓ. Strike across the tussock moor towards the corner of Bunker's Hill Wood. Through a gate there, carry on beside the bounding wall, climbing past the end of Harland Edge to a crossing track at the top corner of the plantation. The prehistoric burial site of Hob Hurst's House then lies only a short distance to the right Ⓔ.

The early Bronze Age burial mound

was first excavated by the Victorian antiquarian Thomas Bateman. Born at nearby Rowsley, he followed his father's interest in archaeology and investigated so many ancient burials that he became known as the 'Barrow Knight'. He opened Hob Hurst's House in 1853 to find fragments of burnt human bones and pieces of lead ore. Unusually, the burial is angular rather than round and the inner chamber, walled with upright slabs, is surrounded by a ditch and earth bank. The beliefs of these ancient peoples have been lost in time, but such monuments demonstrate a reverence for ancestors

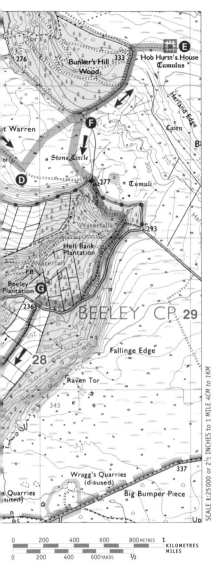

and affirm a belonging to the land.

Hob Hurst is a Derbyshire goblin about whom tales are widespread throughout the Peak. He frequented caves, wooded hollows, stone circles and burial mounds and there are many 'houses' where he supposedly lived. It paid to stay in his good books, for he might then clean the house or ensure the milking went well, but cross him and ill luck was likely to follow. Some folk kept clear of his lairs while others

left appeasing offerings of milk, ale or even a suit of clothes.

Some 300 yds east of the burial is an ancient stone cross or waymark, interesting for the quaint three-fingered hands showing 'Bakewell Road', 'Chesterfeild Road' and 'Sheaffeild Roade'. Unfortunately there is none pointing south, the direction you want, so you must retrace your steps past Hob Hurst's House and follow the wall back down the hill beside the plantation.

Just after passing through the gate and crossing a planked ditch, watch for a fork in the path ●F. Branch left and keep left where it again splits to meet the end of a track (the one you left earlier) at the corner of Hell Bank Plantation. Over a stile beside a gate, cross to another gate opposite, from which a path leads into the trees. At a fork, go left, shortly crossing a stream and reaching a second fork. Now bear right, descending across the wooded slope of the valley. Carry on as a path joins and then, where the way divides, choose the right branch, before long meeting a lane. However, remain in the wood along a path beside the wall, which ultimately leads to a stile ●G.

Cross to the gated track opposite, a bridleway that runs pleasantly between walled fields below Fallinge Edge for ¾ mile. Approaching Fallinge Farm and immediately after a large barn, turn off right along a grass bridleway signed to Rowsley. After only 70 yds, leave over a stile on the right ●H and strike across the field to another stile. A path drops sharply left and then almost immediately right across the steep bank of Smeltingmill Wood. Emerging from the trees, maintain the diagonal across a couple of meadows and then turn down beside the boundary. Reaching the bottom, go right at the foot of a final field onto the lane. Beeley is then just a short walk to the left. ●

Dane Bridge and Lud's Church

		GPS waypoints	
Start	Gradbach	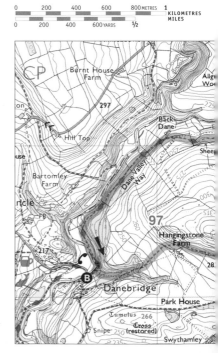 SJ 998 662	
Distance	6¼ miles (10.1km)	**A** SJ 990 657	
Height gain	1,120 feet (341m)	**B** SJ 965 651	
Approximate time	3 hours	**C** SJ 977 653	
Parking	Car park at start	**D** SJ 986 657	
Route terrain	Woodland and field paths	**E** SJ 995 649	
Ordnance Survey maps	Landranger 118 (Stoke-on-Trent & Macclesfield), Explorer OL24 (The Peak District – White Peak area)	**F** SJ 990 656	

The River Dane has its source on the bleak moors of Axe Edge, but quickly delves into a lovely wooded valley between the hills. The walk follows its secretive passage to Dane Bridge, returning over open heath and forest through the darkly impressive, narrow defile of Lud's Church.

Leaving the car park, follow the lane to the right, shortly branching off along a drive to Gradbach Youth Hostel. It sits beside the river in the building of an 18th-century silk mill where there is also a **tearoom** open during weekend afternoons. Swing in front of the main building and then go left onto a short path by the river. Rising to a gate, continue briefly at the field edge before hopping over a stile onto a contained path. Where that then bends sharply left, leave ahead over a stile to a footbridge spanning Black Brook above its confluence with the River Dane **A**.

On the far bank, veer right across a clearing to join a higher path above the main river. There follows a delightful ¾ mile walk through the mixed woodland, heather and bilberry cloaking the steep slope. The river pursues a rocky course, periodically tumbling into short ravines above which, the path has to climb.

Eventually, the way breaks through a gate into open pasture. A clear trod leads past Black Forest Farm, above wooded enclosures, where pigs root, and paddocks containing Soay and Boreray sheep. Keep going from field to field to intercept a track above Back Dane. Bear right, but as it subsequently bends towards the farmhouse, stay ahead, soon delving into more trees. Returning to meadow and once again by the river, carry on to the far end where a track rises to Dane Bridge.

However, just before its end, look for a stile on the left from which a steep path is signed to Hanging Stone **B**. Climb above a deep, wooded gash holding a stream, shortly joining another path from the right and ultimately emerging over a stile. Strike half-left towards Hangingstone Farm, named for the massive outcrop erupting on the hill above. Mounting a stile to the left of the farm, bear right behind the buildings to meet a track.

A sign to the Roaches directs you right. At a junction beyond a cattle-grid, bear left to a gate, from which a

The narrow ravine of Lud's Church

rising path is signed to Gradbach. At another junction **C**, go left, still following Gradbach signs and climbing to a gate at the top of the ridge. Through that, keep ahead now gently losing height across heath from which there is a superb view over the Dane Valley. Entering the birch of Forest Wood, the way soon leads to a fork by a prominent outcrop in a small clearing.

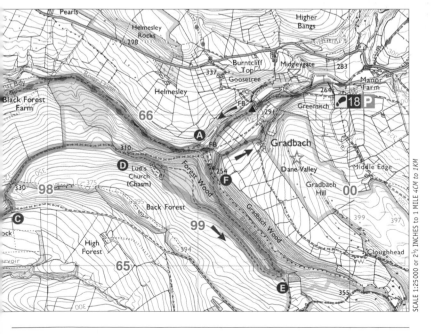

The rocky outcrop in Forest Wood

Branch right towards Lud's Church and then keep an eye open for another turning, not far along on the right 🅓. A path slips through a crack in the sandstone cliff, descending into a deep moss- and fern-draped chasm.

Local legend says that this was the Green Church where Sir Gawain came to face the Green Knight. A year and a day previously, the Green Knight had thrown him a challenge; he would take a single blow from his axe providing Gawain submit to the same. Gawain severed his head, but the knight simply replaced it and walked away. Returning to honour his appointment, Gawain's integrity was tested by the seductive Lady Bertilak. Although he resisted her advances, he accepted a green sash to protect him from harm. When the two knights met, Gawain dutifully bowed before the axe, but the Green Knight merely touched his neck and then revealed himself as the lady's husband. It is said that the Green Knight's head peers from the rocks, so accept no rash challenges on your journey.

Wind through and, as you clamber out at the far end, choose the right branch where a stepped path leads to the top. Carry on between the trees, passing a path off on the right before reaching a T-junction. Turn right, eventually reaching a second junction, from which, a path is signed sharp left to Gradbach 🅔.

After initially dropping steeply, the gradient eases to a fork. Bear left, still slanting across the slope and closing with the stream below at a ford 🅕. There is neither footbridge nor stepping stones, but if the water is low it can be crossed without great difficulty to a rising track. However, the bridge encountered at the start of the walk 🅐, is only a short distance downstream. You can then return either along your outward route, passing the **Riverside Café** at the mill, or climb right beside the wall to meet the track from the ford.

If you managed the ford, follow the track uphill, which soon levels as it leaves the trees. Keep ahead as other tracks join, the way becoming metalled and eventually taking you back to the car park. ●

Biggin and Biggin Dale

		GPS waypoints
Start	Alsop Moor	 SK 157 564
Distance	6½ miles (10.5km)	Ⓐ SK 162 584
Height gain	1,310 feet (399m)	Ⓑ SK 154 588
Approximate time	3½ hours	Ⓒ SK 147 595
Parking	Large lay-by beside A515	Ⓓ SK 142 569
Route terrain	Field paths and tracks	Ⓔ SK 146 561
Ordnance Survey maps	Landranger 119 (Buxton & Matlock), Explorer OL24 (The Peak District – White Peak area)	Ⓕ SK 151 563

The walk begins along the Tissington Trail, taking the high ground to Biggin, where a pub marks the halfway point. The return delves into its pretty namesake dale to meet the River Dove at the foot of Wolfscote Dale before climbing back to the old LNWR trackbed.

From the roadside parking, cross to a gated track opposite that leads to the Tissington Trail. Follow it right. Alternating between high embankments, from which there are fine views to the west, and deep wooded cutting, across which is a high bridge that, despite its grandeur, is merely a link between fields split asunder by the railway, the track meanders through an undulating countryside. Breaking once more into the open, continue over one bridge but approaching a second drop left to the farm track below Ⓐ.

The Tissington Trail follows the course of the former London and North Western Railway line that ran between Ashbourne and Buxton and which operated from 1899 until its final closure in 1967. The Peak Planning Board

in a pioneering project to reopen such routes as leisure trails subsequently purchased the trackbed. Since inauguration in 1971 the trail has been enjoyed by countless people and has become a model for similar schemes right across the country.

Over a stile opposite, take a diagonal course across the fields, later picking up a wall on the left and then joining a

Biggin Dale

track that leads out to the corner of a lane **B**. Turn right into Biggin. Meeting the main road, follow it left past St Thomas's Church and the **Waterloo Inn**. Carry on for a further $^1/_4$ mile to a junction with Harding's Lane. Go right but abandon the road almost immediately for a gated track on the left signed to Biggin Dale **C**.

Biggin evolved around a grange belonging to the medieval Cistercian abbey at Garendon in Leicestershire. Although little remains from that time, the village continues as a farming community and busy sheep markets were run here until the large agricultural centre was opened at Bakewell.

The path falls gently into a descending fold flanked by tall trees on the eastern slope. A feeling of remoteness develops as the way continues beyond a gate into the narrow meadow footing the dale. Lower down, curve left as if to enter the joining side valley. However, passing through a gate, turn right at a sign to Wolfscote Dale to continue along the main valley. The path wanders on through ash and thorn wood, which later thins away and the sound of running water heralds your approach to Wolfscote Dale. Joining a path by the River Dove **D**, follow it downstream through a gate towards Mill Dale.

After $^3/_4$ mile, at Coldeaton Bridge, pass through a gate and then turn off left **E**. Following a wall beside a steeply rising wood, the way becomes progressively rocky as it gains height

A spring breaks out at the foot of Biggin Dale

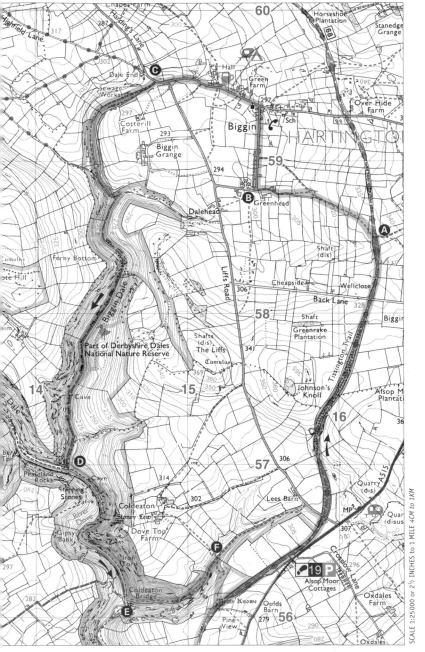

into a deep and narrowing side valley. Towards the top, a gate marks the National Trust boundary of Bradbury's Bank **F**. Instead of passing out, double back right on a trod across the valley slope. Through a gap in the top wall, bear right towards a railway bridge.

Climb the embankment to regain the Tissington Trail and go left, leaving after a little over ¹/₄ mile to return to the lay-by. ●

Langsett and Midhope Reservoirs

Langsett and Midhope Reservoirs

		GPS waypoints
Start	Langsett Reservoir	SE 210 004
Distance	6½ miles (10.5km)	**A** SE 215 001
Height gain	950 feet (290m)	**B** SK 225 997
Approximate time	3 hours	**C** SK 233 986
Parking	Car park at start	**D** SK 213 995
Route terrain	Generally good paths and tracks, quiet lanes	**E** SE 197 000
		F SE 197 006
Ordnance Survey maps	Landranger 110 (Sheffield & Huddersfield), Explorer OL1 (The Peak District – Dark Peak area)	

The Langsett Reservoir is a popular beauty spot and a favourite walk combines the lakeside woods with a return across the moorland flanks of Hingcliff Hill past the ruin of North America Farm. The route suggested here extends it to include a circuit of the adjacent but less-frequented Midhope Reservoir, and gives an opportunity to stride out along a quiet back lane.

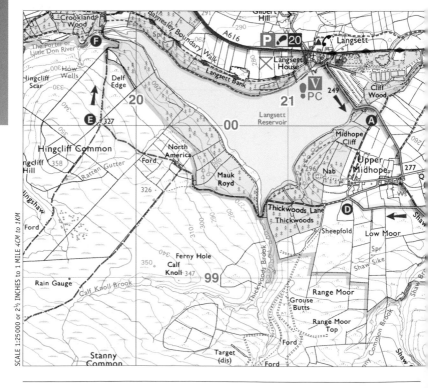

SCALE 1:25000 or 2½ INCHES to 1 MILE 4CM to 1KM

Like many of the Pennine reservoirs, Langsett and Midhope are a direct product of the Industrial Revolution, which spawned a dramatic growth of towns as people came off the land in droves to work in the mills and factories. Together with a treatment plant, both were built to supply water to Sheffield and Barnsley. Langsett, the larger of the two, was begun in 1889 and took almost six years to complete, with Midhope being finished just a little earlier. They exhibit the bold architecture of the time, when public buildings and other works were designed, not only to be functional, but also to emphasise the success and greatness of Empire and the Victorian era. The woods surrounding the reservoirs were a later feature, planted to help stabilise the banks as well as provide a cash crop in the timber they produced. Equally

Descending Hingcliff Hill

important today is their environmental benefit in providing habitats that encourage wildlife, a role that has been helped by more recent replanting using a variety of species.

🥾 Leave the car park past the barn and toilet facilities, winding between the stone cottages beyond to emerge onto the main road by the 19th-century **Waggon and Horses**. Go right and right again along a lane signed to Strines and the Derwent Valley. After crossing the Langsett Dam, follow the lane for another 150 yds to find a track on the right and a waymarked stile on the left **A**.

*The track offers a shortcut through the plantation of Upper Midhope to point **D**, missing out the Midhope Reservoir.* The main route, however, lies over the stile on the left. Head downfield, continuing beyond, by a wall on the left, for a further 150 yds to reach a stone stile. The path slants down through the adjacent woodland strip to run above the Little Don River.

Leave the wood over a stile by a bridge and keep ahead on this bank along a green track. Parting company with the water, it rises to a gate. Carry on at the edge of a field and then a more open area before joining a walled

track that leads out to the bend of a lane. Follow it ahead across the outflow of the Midhope Reservoir, climbing beyond for 100 yds to reach a stile in the wall above **B**.

Head up the field edge and, drawing level with the Midhope dam, pass through a small gate to continue through a larch plantation fringing the water, not identified on the Ordnance Survey Explorer map. A fence later forces the path in an oblique descent to the valley where it then turns from the head of the lake to follow a stream. Watch for the path eventually swinging right and left before leaving the woodland onto a lane **C**.

Go right to a junction and then right again, the way signed to Upper Midhope and Langsett. The lane runs back above the trees bordering the southern shore of the lake, dipping after one mile across Shaw Brook, the main catchment stream for the reservoir. Shortly the lane swings left, rising to a sharp right-hand bend and junction of tracks **D**.

Take the concrete track off left, keeping ahead at its end through a gate into Thickwoods. Roughly paved, a relic

of its wartime use to train tank crews in the run up to the D-Day landings, the track inconsiderately gives up the height you have so far gained, dropping to an inlet where Thickwoods Brook enters the Langsett Reservoir. After winding back to cross the stream climb away from the lake above Mauk Royd Wood, eventually passing through a gate onto the upper moor. Carry on past the evocative ruins of North America Farm, whose standing doorjambs are reminiscent of a prehistoric henge. It was one of several in the valley that were cleared when the reservoir was built to ensure the purity of the water. The gradient now eases as the path meanders across Hingcliff Common, topping out at a junction of paths **E**.

The path to the right falls towards the head of the Langsett Reservoir, twisting lower down to mollify the final steepness as it drops to a bridge across the Little Don River **F**. Climb away on a broad path, leaving after the initial pull along a gravelled, waymarked path on the right. It weaves easily through the trees above the full length of the lake. Fragmenting at the far end, the middle branch takes you directly back up to the car park. ●

The Porter or Little Don River

Crowden and Millstone Rocks

Start	Crowden	**GPS waypoints**	
Distance	6½ miles (10.5km)	🖉 SK 072 992	
Height gain	1,550 feet (472m)	Ⓐ SK 060 986	
Approximate time	3½ hours	Ⓑ SK 055 981	
Parking	Car park at start	Ⓒ SK 044 979	
Route terrain	Good tracks beside reservoir, clear but peaty upland paths, *take care in mist*	Ⓓ SK 044 992	
		Ⓔ SK 067 995	
Ordnance Survey maps	Landranger 110 (Sheffield & Huddersfield), Explorer OL1 (The Peak District – Dark Peak area)		

Once part of a royal hunting forest, Longdendale now cradles a chain of reservoirs that stretches for more than 5½ miles (8.9km). This superb walk follows the two middle lakes and then climbs back above the valley to the spectacular vantage of Millstone Rocks, which looks out across Longdendale and its southern escarpments to the moorland expanse of Bleaklow. The return is no less dramatic, with glimpses into the twin valleys of Crowden Brook.

🖉 Leave the far end of the car park towards the toilets, there turning right on a path beside the campsite, which leads to a junction at the entrance to a farm. Through a gate to the left, a track leads past the farm and over a bridge spanning Crowden Brook. The two arms of the stream cleave deep valleys that bite into the lonely upland moors, which rise to Black Hill, one of the highest points of the Peak. The onward track then begins to climb, cresting the rise beside a plantation of pine. Falling beyond, a view opens across the Torside Reservoir along whose far bank once ran the Sheffield, Ashton under Lyne & Manchester Railway. Plainly visible is the embankment, which took it across the foot of Torside Clough, a deep cleft in the escarpment along which the Pennine

Way is routed off Bleaklow Head.

The Woodhead railway between Manchester and Sheffield was the first to be pushed across the Pennines and opened in 1845. The tunnel, upon which the line depended, took almost eight years to complete and, at just over 3 miles, was then one of the world's longest. The enterprise was an immediate success and within seven years a second tunnel enabling two-way working was opened to accommodate increasing traffic. At one point around 500 steam trains a day were passing through. However, steep gradients and smoke pollution within the tunnels were continuing problems. Work began on electrification in 1936, but was disrupted by the war. It also became clear that the existing tunnels were too small and could

Past Crowden Quarries to Woodhead

not be adapted to carry the overhead wires. In consequence, a third tunnel, this time two-way, was dug. It saw its first trains in 1953 and remained in use until the line was closed in 1981. They are now owned by the National Grid, who use one of the Victorian tunnels to take the trans-Pennine power cables beneath the summit, thus protecting them from the severe winter weather on the tops. The cables are shortly due for replacement and it was planned to re-lay them through the 'new' tunnel. However, there is pressure to re-open the route to carry freight and help alleviate trans-Pennine road traffic, and at the moment, its future remains uncertain.

Reaching the main road **A**, cross to a path opposite, which descends right to meander through a strip of plantation above the lake. Through a gate at the far end of the wood, drop to cross a service track and continue down steps to another track below. Follow it across the top of the Torside Dam to find a waymarked dirt track leaving through a gate on the right **B**. Running below the course of the railway, it soon emerges from trees to give a view along Rhodeswood Reservoir, unfortunately compromised by striding pylons carrying one of the main trans-Pennine

electricity supplies. At a fork beyond a stile, bear right, the way losing height to the dam at the foot of the lake **C**.

Walk back to the northern bank and carry on up the service drive to the main road. Through a gate opposite, follow a rough track onto the heather-clad hillside. Stay with it around a sharp right bend and then keep left at a fork. Later bend left, pass another junction and then bend sharp right. Continue to a stile and gate into the upper part of the Didsbury Intake plantation. The track pursues its

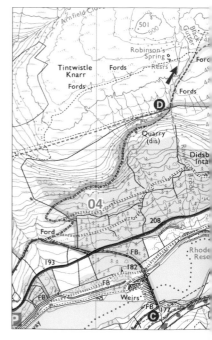

rising plod through the trees, eventually levelling below the cliffs of an old quarry. Where the track ends, carry on along a path, climbing across the fractured face before eventually turning up to reach a stile at the top beside the peaty runnel of Rawkins Brook **D**.

Crossing the stream, pick up a rough path that strikes north east across the moss towards the higher ground, some $^1/_4$ mile distant. Wet weather might sometimes have you casting around for firm going, but in late summer the purple expanse of flowering heather is more than ample compensation. The way rises to the top of an outcrop, Millstone Rocks, which stands above the impressive rocky amphitheatre of Coombes Clough.

The path, now improved underfoot initially follows the rim, before turning in above the ravine to guide you to a convenient crossing point. Clambering away at the far side the path drifts back from the edge as it begins a gradual descent across the moor. Over to the left, peeping above the horizon is the

mast of the Holme Moss transmitter, rather deceptively only 4 miles away. As the intermediate ground falls away, the view opens to the twin valleys of Crowden Brook, which find their source on the bleak upper slopes of Black Hill. Beyond the end of a broken wall, the route falls along a shallow trough then accompanies another wall down the hill. Ahead, extensive quarries high on the abrupt nose of Hey Moss overlook the foot of the Woodhead Reservoir, the highest of the series that cascade down the valley.

At the bottom corner of the wall, cross a stile and continue steeply down the hillside towards a farm, soon reaching a junction of paths beside a small memorial copse of trees **E**. Turn through the small gate on the right and follow the boundary away across successive enclosures to emerge onto the track along which the walk began. Go left back to the car park. ●

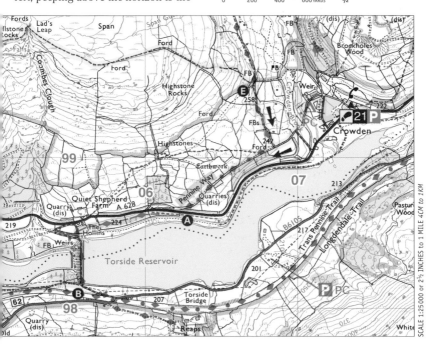

Grindon and the River Hamps

		GPS waypoints
Start	Grindon	📷 SK 085 544
Distance	7½ miles (12.1km)	**Ⓐ** SK 098 550
Height gain	1,500 feet (457m)	**Ⓑ** SK 100 541
Approximate time	4 hours	**Ⓒ** SK 093 515
Parking	Car park by church	**Ⓓ** SK 084 517
Route terrain	Field paths and valley trails	**Ⓔ** SK 083 519
Ordnance Survey maps	Landranger 119 (Buxton & Matlock), Explorer OL24 (The Peak District – White Peak area)	

Most of the White Peak's drainage tends south easterly, but the River Hamps is an exception, forced north in a great loop from Waterhouses to meet the River Manifold at Beeston Tor. This walk follows part of its course along the disused line of the Manifold Light Railway, returning to Grindon across the high plateau pastures from which there are fine views to the Staffordshire Moorland. But first, there is an opportunity to visit Thor's Cave, the most dramatic site in the Manifold Valley.

All Saints' is known as the 'Cathedral of the Moorlands' and was founded as a chapel of ease to Ilam in the 11th century. Reminders of the early building are to be found in the Saxon font, a window panel of medieval glass and a pair of massive charnel coffins, once used to store old bones unearthed when reopening graves. An embroidered memorial remembers eight men who died in 1947 when a Halifax of 47 Squadron crashed on Grindon Moor in an attempt to drop much-needed food supplies. The upland villages had been cut off for several weeks by deep snow during an exceptionally severe winter. The weather closed in as the plane arrived and, in trying to locate the drop zone, it hit the ground killing six crew members and two news photographers.

Ironically, the road to Leek was opened later the same day. Outside the church is a pillar inscribed with a curious inscription, 'Lord of the Manor of Grindon established his right to this rindle at the Staffordshire Assizes on 17 March 1862', a rindle being a local word for a stream that flows only after rain.

📷 From the south gate of All Saints' Church, follow the lane past the old rectory. Beyond more houses, leave along a short, signed track on the left. Head straight out across a field, making for the right-hand one of two stiles in an intervening fence. Drop to a footbridge spanning a tiny stream and bear right to a wicket gate. Continue along the flank of a deepening valley, passing onto the National Trust land of Ladyside. After angling above the

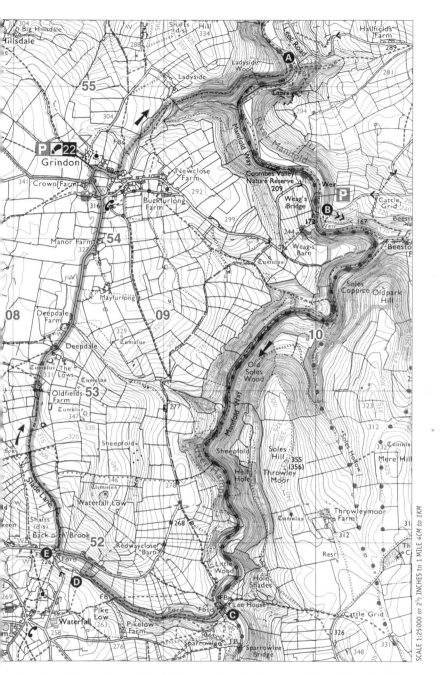

almost precipitous slope of the valley, the path passes through woodland before dropping more steeply beside open scrub to the River Manifold **A**.

Opposite rears a stark limestone cliff, rent by the great gape of Thor's Cave, the climb to which is less arduous than it appears. Cross the bridge and follow a rising path into the trees. At a signpost part-way up, turn sharp right, and continue up steps, shortly reaching the

SCALE 1:25000 or 2½ INCHES to 1 MILE 4CM to 1KM

0	200	400	600	800 METRES	1
					KILOMETRES
					MILES
0	200	400	600 YARDS	½	

All Saints' and the Grindon Rindle stone

mouth of the cave.

Return to cross the bridge and now turn left down the Manifold. The broad trail in time leads to a lane at Weags Bridge **B**. Cross the lane to the right-hand one of the parallel tracks opposite and continue along the valley, shortly reaching a small farm campsite below Beeston Tor. Here, the track discretely abandons the Manifold, turning up into the narrower confines of the Hamps valley.

Like parts of the Manifold, the River Hamps often disappears below ground and, unless there has been particularly heavy rain, you are unlikely to see water in the gorge. The trail still follows the former railway, crossing from bank to bank above the rocky river bed. After two mile's easy walking, the valley broadens at Woodhead Farm, where there is a **tearoom** and garden.

Just beyond, cross the river for a final time and then quit the trail through a kissing-gate on the right **C**. Walk up a meadow into a narrowing side valley. Reaching a stile on the right, cross and continue by the fence, the bed of the accompanying brook perhaps now running with water. Carry on to a bridge **D**, but ignore that and instead cross a stile on the right. Climb steeply to a stile at the top of the field.

To the left, a lane drops to a sharp bend above a ford in front of Brookhouse Farm **E**. Leave at that point, turning right through a couple of gates along a climbing, sunken track, Slade Lane. Eventually, beyond another gate, it peters out into a field, but carry on by the right-hand boundary. Through more gates the way soon develops as a field track that tops out at Oldfields Farm. Approaching the farm, choose the left-hand one of two adjacent gates, passing through yard to leave along a metalled track. After a leisurely ¾ mile walk, it leads to a junction in Grindon, overlooked by what used to be the Cavalier Inn. Keep ahead and then fork right to return to the church.

The Cavalier remembers Bonnie Prince Charlie's foray into Derbyshire, before returning with his Jacobite army to Scotland where it was butchered by the Duke of Cumberland at the Battle of Culloden in 1746. Charles reputedly stayed in the village and some of his followers apparently abandoned the cause and settled in the area. ●

Edale and Crookstone Hill

Start	Edale	**GPS waypoints**	
Distance	7¾ miles (12.5km)	🔲 SK 123 853	
Height gain	1,700 feet (518m)	Ⓐ SK 122 861	
		Ⓑ SK 122 862	
Approximate time	4 hours	Ⓒ SK 125 875	
Parking	Car park at start (Pay and Display)	Ⓓ SK 143 880	
Route terrain	Moorland paths, *take care in mist*	Ⓔ SK 153 879	
		Ⓕ SK 159 876	
Ordnance Survey maps	Landranger 110 (Sheffield & Huddersfield), Explorer OL1 (The Peak District – Dark Peak area)	Ⓖ SK 133 859	

While the Kinder Plateau might seem an inhospitable wilderness, its edges, by contrast, are full of interest and offer spectacular views every step of the way. Beginning at Edale, this trek explores the south-eastern corner and descends the long nose of Crookstone Hill before returning along gentle slopes flanking the Vale of Edale.

🔲 Leaving the car park by the **toilets**, turn beneath the railway and head up through the village, passing **The Old Nag's Head**. Continue beyond as the lane becomes a track, but, reaching the lodge and gate to Grindslow House Ⓐ, drop right to a bridge across Grinds Brook. Above the far bank, briefly follow a causey to a small stone barn Ⓑ. Leave it there, branching right on a grass path rising to a gate.

From it, a zigzagging, stepped path tackles the steep slope of the valley side, swapping views across the valley to the Mam Tor ridge for those into the far recesses of Grindsbrook Clough. Veer right when the steps finish to stay on the main path and then go left as the gradient eventually eases on the nose of The Nab. At a large cairn below the ragged cliffs of Ringing Roger, bear left and follow the path through the heather into Golden Clough.

Particularly in winter, these harsh uplands might appear devoid of life, but

keep your eyes and ears open and you'll discover that many creatures make a living here. Perhaps most obvious are the birds, some like the skylark appearing with the spring, but others, including the grouse, sitting out the winter too. They feed off the heather, which is regularly burnt to encourage new growth. Also common are mountain hares, which in winter assume a white coat to aid its camouflage when the snow falls. Fleet footed, they bound up the slopes with ease, but are prey to predatory hawks such as the peregrine, which is making a comeback. Tiny voles are secretive, but you could just be lucky enough to spot one scurrying across the path into the grass. During warm weather, you might also come across small lizards sunning themselves on the rock.

Approaching the top, remain on this bank of the stream gully, soon intercepting a slabbed, crossing path Ⓒ. To the right, it undulates easily

Grindsbrook Clough

into Jaggers Clough. Jaggers were the men who led teams of packhorses along the trails across the moors, the only way that goods could be carried across rough country before the introduction of the turnpike roads in the 18th century. A short but sharp climb inevitably follows, but the track soon resumes a gentle descent towards Clough Farm. Approaching the farm, watch for a footpath branching off right, which is

across the high moor, cutting across the neck of the spur out to Ringing Roger. The stone flags finish at a fence stile, but the path remains clear, gently curving left to a second stile by the corner of another fence. Keep going around the head of Ollerbrook Clough and then above Rowland Cote Moor, enjoying the far-reaching views along the valley to Win Hill Pike and Derwent Edge beyond. After dipping to cross the stream feeding Jaggers Clough, the way begins to lose height, picking up a crumbling wall on your right. When it ends, watch for a fork **D** and take the right branch, which descends more pronouncedly. Later, cross a stile beside a gate to leave the open moor, continuing along a grass track to a pair of sycamore trees starkly prominent in splendid isolation **E**.

An unusual stone waypost directs you left on a narrower but clear path towards Hope Cross, before long meeting a broad gravel path. Follow it right through a gate, soon reaching a crossing of paths in front of a second gate **F**. Hope Cross stands just a little way ahead and is worth visiting if only to see the quaint spellings of the places depicted on its four faces.

The way back to Edale, however, lies to the right, crossing the long snout of Crookstone Hill before dropping steeply

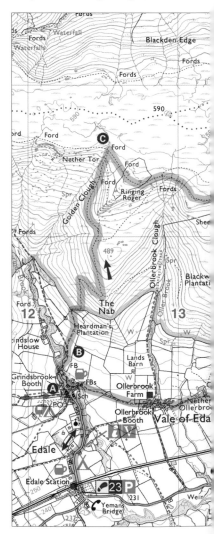

signed to the Edale Youth Hostel. It traces the boundary of the access land above the farm, turning in to cross the stream that drops off the hill behind.

Eventually the path swings again above Lady Booth Brook, bringing the gabled red roof of the youth hostel into view. Cross the stream and go left, joining the drive past the front of the building. Walk on to a gate at the far side of the parking area and continue on a grass path across the slope of the hill. Keep going from field to field, eventually passing above a small wood. Curve down beyond its end to meet a gravel path **G**.

Follow it right through a gate to Nether Ollerbrook. There, a track leads past the buildings, but as that then swings left, a sign to Edale directs you forward through a gate by a small red post box. Walk through a yard and on across more fields. Where the track later curves right, keep ahead, dropping to a pretty stone bridge spanning Grinds Brook. Emerging in the village beside the pub, go left back to the car park. ●

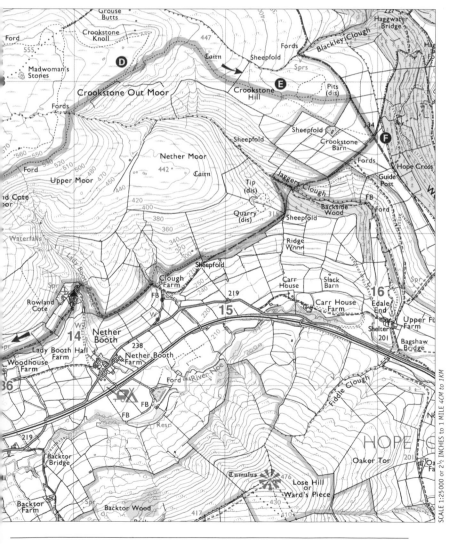

SCALE 1:25 000 or 2½ INCHES to 1 MILE 4CM to 1KM

Win Hill and Hope Cross

		GPS waypoints	
Start	Ashopton	🥾	SK 202 858
Distance	8¼ miles (13.3km)	Ⓐ	SK 198 856
Height gain	1,590 feet (485m)	Ⓑ	SK 193 851
Approximate time	4 hours	Ⓒ	SK 186 850
Parking	Heatherdene car park	Ⓓ	SK 161 874
Route terrain	Clear tracks and paths through forest and upland grazing	Ⓔ	SK 163 878
Ordnance Survey maps	Landranger 110 (Sheffield & Huddersfield), Explorer OL1 (The Peak District – Dark Peak area)		

After an initial climb through forest plantations overlooking the Ladybower Dam to the craggy height of Win Hill, there follows a superb, view-filled saunter on a broad, grassy ridge over Wooler Knoll. Dropping into the Ashop Valley the return undulates along the full length of the western arm of the reservoir.

🥾 From the southern corner of the lower car park, follow a path past the toilets signed to the Ladybower Dam. Coming level with the dam, drop to the road, where there is a monument listing the worthies of the Water Board when the dam was opened by King George VI on 25 September 1945.

Although begun ten years earlier, the dam's construction had been hampered by the war and it was not completed until 1943, with a further two years being required for it to fill up. Unlike the dams higher up the valley, it is not built of solid masonry, but is a massive earthen embankment waterproofed with a clay core sat upon a concrete foundation that extends deep into the hills to prevent water seeping around the side. Fifty years of use inevitably took their toll and during the 1990s the dam underwent a major refurbishment. This included the provision of a pathway across the top of the 650-foot (594m) dam, which has opened new options for walks in the area, such as this one.

Follow the footpath across the dam, turning right along the bridleway on the far side. Abandon it after 200 yds for a rising path into the trees signed off to New Barn Ⓐ. The path heralds a steady ascent across the slope of the hill. Emerging through a gate onto a broader path, go left, the way still rising albeit more gently. Keep going for a good ½ mile, eventually meeting a path coming up along Parkin Clough Ⓑ. To the right, a stepped path makes a direct attack on the hillside, ending through a gate at another junction of paths.

Take the one diagonally opposite, signed to Win Hill, which climbs on through Winhill Plantation. Breaking cover, pass through a gap in a wall for the final pull onto the tor crowning Win Hill Ⓒ.

With the reservoirs below your feet and hills all around, the view is extensive. Across the water is the tor-studded line of Derwent Edge, while in the other direction across the Noe Valley is Lose Hill, otherwise known as

The Ladybower Reservoir from Winhill Pike

Ward's Piece, the culmination of a long ridge of hills dividing the Vale of Edale from the Hope Valley. As the walk unfolds, the eye is later drawn along Edale and to the high plateau of Kinder, overshadowing it from the north.

Having taken your fill of the panorama, drop to the path below the summit rocks and head west in a gentle descent. Eventually, as the accompanying boundary is left behind, the path arcs right and assumes the line of the ridge, re-opening the view across Ladybower before it closes with the plantation boundary beyond Wooler Knoll. Watch for the path later curving left to meet a lower track, the line of the Roman road linking two forts, Navio beside the River Noe and Melandra near Glossop. Passing through a gate, it runs for ¹/₂ mile to Hope Cross **D**. The 18th-century waymark stands at a junction of ancient trails, its square crown indicating the direction and destination of each (notice the unusual rendering of 'Shefield').

Through the gate just beyond, immediately turn right over a stile into the forest. Bearing left, a dark path drops for ¹/₄ mile through the trees to emerge in a small clearing by the ruin of a building. Turn right (not sharp right) on a path falling steeply straight down the hill, winding at the bottom to meet a broad forest track at the head of the western arm of the Ladybower Reservoir **E**. To the right, it undulates above the shore for 3 miles to return you to the dam at the foot of the lake.

The Ladybower Reservoir lies at the meeting of two of the Derwent's tributaries; the River Ashop, which has its source on the watershed of the Snake Pass, and the much smaller Ladybower Brook which tumbles from the east and gives the lake its name. When completed in 1943, the reservoir was the largest man-made body of water in Britain, extending over 242 acres (98 hectares). Ladybower was the third in the chain of reservoirs now filling the upper valley

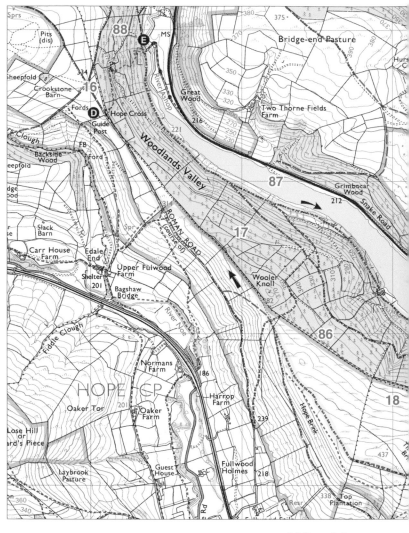

The Ladybower overflow

and followed the completion of the Howden and Derwent water supply reservoirs some 30 years earlier. The rising waters flooded two small villages; Derwent, part-way up the northern arm and Ashopton, which overlooked the confluence with the River Ashop. The villagers were re-housed and their cottages razed and even the dead were exhumed from Derwent's

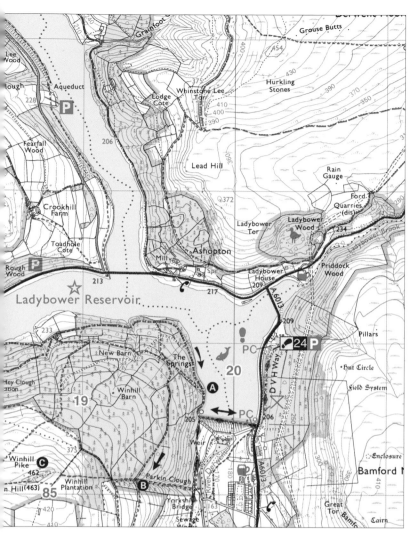

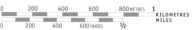

small churchyard for reburial in nearby Bamford. Only the church spire was left intact, an intended memorial to the village, but by 1947 that too had been demolished.

The Ladybower Reservoir was built, not only to extend the water supply capability of the area, but also to help maintain a consistent flow in the River Derwent below the dam. When river levels drop, water is released from the reservoir to protect the environment and wildlife dependent upon it. One, or perhaps two, unusual features are the circular, bell-mouth shafts located at either side near the foot of the lake. They act as giant plug holes to prevent the reservoir overflowing and channel the excess water into the River Derwent at the base of the dam. The reservoirs collectively hold some 10.5 billion gallons (47.8 million cubic metres) of water and satisfy around 10% of the East Midlands' needs, supplying water to the cities and surrounding areas of Derby, Leicester, Nottingham and Sheffield.

Dovestone Edge

		GPS waypoints
Start	Binn Green	SE 017 043
Distance	9¼ miles (14.9km)	**A** SE 019 045
Height gain	1,750 feet (533m)	**B** SE 037 049
Approximate time	4½ hours	**C** SE 031 044
Parking	Car park beside A635, 1½ miles (2.4km) east of Greenfield	**D** SE 035 019
Route terrain	A short scramble onto the upper moor, with faint paths along the edge, *take care in mist. Clear tracks around the lower reservoirs offer an alternative walk in poor weather*	**E** SE 025 023
		F SE 018 031
Ordnance Survey maps	Landranger 110 (Sheffield & Huddersfield), Explorer OL1 (The Peak District – Dark Peak area)	

An abrupt rocky escarpment defines the western perimeter of Dove Stone Moss overlooking the head of the Tame Valley. From below it presents a dramatic and forbiddingly steep slope, littered with ragged boulders arrested in unruly descent. Then, striding out along the rim, a parapet of shattered, weatherworn cliffs, a sequence of breathtaking views unfolds. The scrambling ascent of Birchen Clough can present a challenge when the stream is in spate, but once accomplished, the remainder of the route is not difficult.

Beside an information board in the car park, a stepped path descends through conifers to a service track. The track drops to the western end of the Yeoman Hey Dam **A**. Carry on above the bank of the lake, taking either branch where the track subsequently splits, since both lead to the higher dam of the Greenfield Reservoir.

The ongoing track continues into an ever-narrowing valley, the steep flank strewn with the debris from the crumbling escarpment above. Beyond the head of the lake, the track dogs the tumbling course of Greenfield Brook, crossing to its southern bank before rising to a turning area at the confluence of two higher ravines **B**.

*The route lies up that to the right, Birchen Clough, and involves fording the stream a couple of times, not always easy after heavy rain. Should you be defeated, you can rescue the day with a perambulation of the chain of lakes. Return to the foot of the Greenfield Reservoir and drop below the dam to pick up a rough path along the eastern shore of Yeoman Hey. Re-cross on its dam to point **A** and go to the left, leaving the service road through a gate just a short way up on the left. The ongoing path runs above the shore of Dovestone and then swings across its much larger retaining dam. Continue around the southern shore past the sailing club to rejoin the main route at*

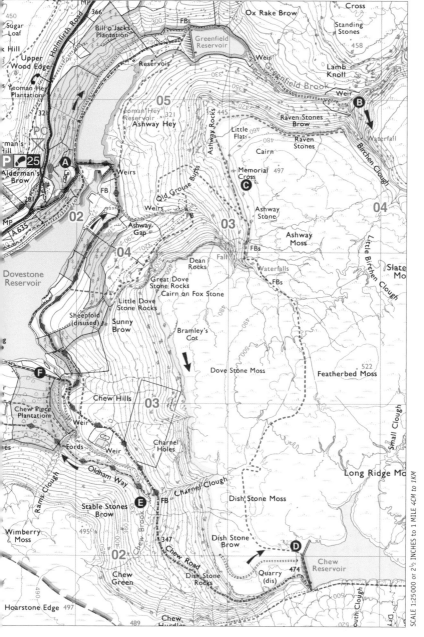

SCALE 1:25 000 or 2½ INCHES to 1 MILE 4CM to 1KM

0 200 400 600 800 METRES 1
KILOMETRES
MILES
0 200 400 600 YARDS ½

the foot of Chew Brook, point **F**.

To join the stream up Birchen Clough, skirt above the tunnel portal of the fenced aqueduct on the right. The 1,260-yard (1152m) tunnel bypasses the two upper reservoirs and was built to preserve water supplies to the mills lower down in the valley. With no obvious path, you must clamber over the boulders beside the stream, shortly switching to the other bank. Higher up as the gradient eases above a small cascade, re-cross to find a slanting path doubling back along the flank of the gorge.

Rising easily to the lip, it continues above the escarpment, revealing a distant panorama across the emptiness of the Saddleworth moors. The jagged rocks immediately below grab attention too, the most impressive being the Trinnacle, a detached three-pronged pillar of stone. Its ascent is reserved for experienced scramblers with a good head for heights and remember that getting up is not necessarily the hardest part of the exercise.

Carry on along the edge, revelling in the tremendous views opening along the valley as you round the headland above Ashway Rocks. A little farther on and set back to the left is the ornately carved Ashway Cross **C**. Now much battered by the elements, it is a memorial to James Platt who was killed in a shooting accident on the moors in 1857, shortly after his election as MP for Oldham.

Stride on above the narrowing clough of Ashway Gap, crossing its head and doubling back along the other side. The airy way runs on over Great Dove Stone Rocks, which tower over the reservoir and, on a good day, the temptation is to linger for the view. Maintain height above the long, climbing valley of Chew Brook, eventually swinging east across the moor to meet the northern end of the Chew Reservoir Dam **D**.

Located almost 1,600 feet (488m) above sea level, it was the highest reservoir in the country when it was built in 1912. Since 1971, the record has been held by the much larger but barely higher Cow Green Reservoir, which stands at the head of Teesdale.

Walk across the dam and turn down the service track into the valley, passing a small quarry, which provided stone for the project. One mile's walking brings you to a bridge at the foot of Charnel Clough **E**. Turn off immediately before it, dropping to a

wooden footbridge across Chew Brook. The ongoing path follows the bed of a tramway along which more than 40,000 tonnes of clay was hauled up the valley to waterproof the dam. Before long the way dips to ford the stream out of Rams Clough, where the stone abutments of the trestle bridge that carried the track are still visible. Over a stile just beyond, fork off onto a lesser path, which falls through Chew Piece Plantation to meet the broad path encircling the Dovestone Reservoir **F**. To the right, it winds pleasantly back to the Yeoman Hey Dam. Cross and retrace your steps to the car park.

Towards the head of the Dovestone Reservoir, below the path, is the site of Ashway Gap House. It was an impressive Gothic-style hunting lodge, built by John Platt, elder brother of James whose memorial was passed on the ridge above. The family's money and prominent local standing derived from an engineering business founded by their father Henry, who began producing textile machinery at Dobcross in 1770. The business rapidly expanded and by the middle of the 19th century had become the largest such company in the world. The lodge was built in 1850 to host grouse shoots on the moor, but following the tragic death of James, John's passion for the sport evaporated and the house lapsed into disuse. The valley estate was eventually acquired by the Ashton, Duckinfield and Stalybridge Waterworks in 1905, whose marker stones of ownership can still be seen on the hillside, and, for a time, the house was used for board meetings. During two World Wars it served as a hospital and subsequently a detention centre for Italian prisoners of war. It was finally demolished in 1981, and a levelling of ground, short flight of garden steps and clump of rhododendron bushes are all that is left now. ●

Alport Castles

		GPS waypoints	
Start	Fairholmes National Park Centre	 SK 172 893	
Distance	8¼ miles (13.3km)	**A** SK 165 896	
Height gain	1,950 feet (594m)	**B** SK 164 890	
Approximate time	4½ hours	**C** SK 141 915	
Parking	Car park at start (Pay and Display)	**D** SK 145 913	
Route terrain	Clear tracks and upland paths	**E** SK 136 909	
Ordnance Survey maps	Landranger 110 (Sheffield & Huddersfield), Explorer OL1 (The Peak District – Dark Peak area)	**F** SK 141 895	
		G SK 151 892	

Alport Castles is one of the spectacular natural features of the northern Peak, standing sentinel above a long and lovely glen. After climbing steeply through the forests of the neighbouring Derwent Valley, there is a grand, scenic walk out across the airy tops of Rowlee Pasture. The return falls along the picturesque valley to the River Ashop before climbing once more over the intervening shoulder back into Derwent.

Leaving the Fairholmes car park by the vehicle exit, cross the road to a gated path opposite. Following signs to Lockerbrook, climb along a wooded side

Birchin Hat

valley past the embankment of a disused railway, laid to bring materials for the construction of the Derwent and Howden dams. Crossing a conduit, fork left and continue upwards to meet a foresters' track. Go left, but shortly after a sharp right bend, abandon it for another path, doubling back on the left. Carry on up through the trees and then at the edge of open pasture, ultimately intersecting a crossing track **A**.

Go left, soon passing Lockerbrook Farm and then climbing beside more trees. Reaching a junction on the top of the rise **B**, strike off right to a ladder-stile on the skyline. Head away along a meadow, scaling a stile at the far side onto the open hillside of Rowlee Pasture.

Progression across the heights of Rowlee Pasture reveals a succession of superb views. The elongated ridge stretching back from Lose Hill to Mam

Tor and Lord's Seat lies back to the left while closer to are the steep abutments defending the desolate wilderness of the Kinder Scout plateau. Over to the right is the deep, long fold of the Derwent Valley, above which the Derwent Edge bristles with rocky outcrops, distinct even from here. Lost Lad, Back Tor and, farther north, Margery Hill are all identifiable, while in front, the moor rises to distant Bleaklow Head, the second highest of the Peakland hills.

The onward way rises in a steady plod, later becoming flagged as it encounters wetter ground. Finally broaching the hill, the fractured crags of Alport Castles appear ahead, though still a good $\frac{1}{2}$ mile away. The path continues above the lip of the chaos of cliffs, reaching a junction at the far end by the corner of a collapsed stone wall **C**.

Alport Castles are the result of a massive and ongoing landslip, one of the largest active geological features in the country. As at Mam Tor, the hard gritstone is layered with bands of soft shale, which has become degraded by the action of moisture and frost. Water seepage acts as a lubricant within the weakened strata, which eventually becomes unstable and slips, bringing down the hillside. The major event occurred following the thaw at the end of the last Ice Age, some 12,000 years ago, creating the great detached islands of rock slumped below the rim. But the cliff face is still vulnerable and heavy rain contributes to ongoing movement and periodic rock falls. Grassed hillocks, shattered faces and aprons of rubble create a confused and spectacular scene, the largest clump of rock resembling the motte of a stark castle, topped with a towering keep.

In contrast to many of the Dark Peak's edges, *the crumbling cliffs are too dangerous for climbing.* Consequently undisturbed and relatively inaccessible

to predators, they have become attractive nesting sites to both raven and peregrine falcon. The biggest of the crow family, the raven is unmistakable; completely black and having a wingspan that can extend to 5 feet (1.5m). They build large, untidy nests that might be used year after year and lay anything up to six eggs in a clutch. Once persecuted almost to the point of extinction, Peregrines are now making a comeback and, although favouring secluded locations such as this, also nest on the ledges of high buildings in towns and cities. Particularly striking is the courtship ritual played out in March

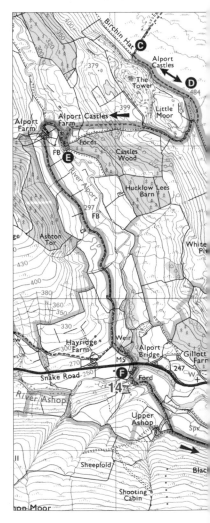

or early April, when pairs can be seen wheeling together in lavish acrobatic displays. In the past, a temporary hide has been erected allowing birdwatchers to observe the chicks in the nest.

Retrace your steps above the landslip for about 500 yds to find a path dropping into a grassy gully **D**. Picking up a boundary, follow it downhill, later crossing a stile and swinging below the boulder debris. Shortly, the way turns steeply downwards once more, accompanying a fence line down to a bridge across the River Alport **E**. Head briefly upstream to find a stile on the left. Cross a small field to emerge at Castles Farm.

A track saunters along the valley towards the main road, just over one mile away. At a bend towards the end, watch for a path leaving on the left. Over a stile, it continues through trees above the river, soon meeting the road beside Alport Bridge **F**.

A sign to Hope and Edale directs you through a gate opposite to a footbridge spanning the River Ashop. On the far bank, bear left along a rough track that rises onto Blackley Hey. Passing below Upper Ashop Farm, join its metalled access and carry on at the edge of the moor along the valley side. Keep left where it later bends past the path to Hope, dropping once more across the river before rising to the road **G**.

Take the track opposite, which, beyond Rowlee Farm, makes a steep zigzagging ascent of the hillside. After running below the crags of Bellhag Tor, the way leads to the junction at the top of the ridge passed on the outward journey **B**.

Rather than retrace your original route, leave immediately beyond the junction over a stile on the right. A path, signed to Fairholmes drops into the forest. Continue down the hillside, but towards the bottom, look for a path signed off left from the main trail. It drops out to the road just south of the Fairholmes car park. ●

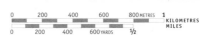

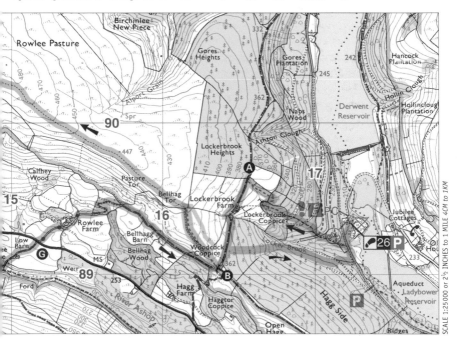

Kinder Low

		GPS waypoints
Start	Hayfield	SK 036 869
Distance	10½ miles (16.9km)	Ⓐ SK 040 868
Height gain	2,180 feet (664m)	Ⓑ SK 049 883
Approximate time	5½ hours	Ⓒ SK 063 900
Parking	Car park at former railway station (Pay and Display)	Ⓓ SK 083 889
		Ⓔ SK 078 870
Route terrain	Steep rocky and moorland paths, *take care in mist*	Ⓕ SK 080 861
		Ⓖ SK 051 867
Ordnance Survey maps	Landranger 110 (Sheffield & Huddersfield), Explorer OL1 (The Peak District – Dark Peak area)	

The ascent of Kinder Low ranks high among the popular walks in the Peak, but avoid bank holidays and summer weekends and you can still appreciate its lonely grandeur. Leaving Hayfield the route follows the Snake Path onto Mill Hill and then turns up onto the rim of the Kinder Scout plateau. There follows a glorious 2½ mile traverse of the edge past Kinder Downfall to Kinder Low, before dropping from the high moor to return along an old packhorse trail. Inexperienced walkers are advised not to attempt the walk in poor visibility, for the path leaving Kinder Low is faint and can be confusing in mist.

Leaving the car park occupying Hayfield's former railway station, cross the main road at the traffic lights. Walk beside the church into town and go left over the River Sett. Just beyond, turn right up Bank Street, joining Kinder Road. After ¼ mile, as the gradient eases, look for a track signed off left to the **Snake Inn Ⓐ**.

Resume your ascent, climbing past an isolated copse and soon abandoning the fields for the open moor. Keep going, before long reaching a junction below some white-painted shooting huts **Ⓑ**. Stay ahead, falling gently to a fork. Bear left to contour the steep side of White Brow above the Kinder Reservoir. Towards the far end of the lake, the path drops, picking up a lower path to follow

the stream into William Clough. The rift quickly narrows, leaving little room for the path, which hops, from one bank to the other in search of the best route. At a fork towards the top, keep right with the main branch, which improves underfoot towards the Mill Hill saddle. Approaching the crest, watch for a paved path leaving the Snake Path on the right **Ⓒ**. If you miss it, there is a distinct waymark at a cross-path, just a few yards farther on.

The route onto Kinder follows in the footsteps of the famous Kinder Trespass, which left the small quarry at Bowden Bridge on Sunday 24 April 1932. The march was led by Benny Rothman, a Socialist and lover of the outdoors, who often found himself out of work because of his politics. The day had been well advertised and some 400 people took part in the protest against the landowners' prohibition of access to the moor. The scheme was to meet up on the top of Kinder Scout with a Sheffield group starting from Edale. The crowd was in good spirits as they ascended William Clough and it was not until they began climbing onto the high moor that they encountered the gamekeepers. Apart from a few scuffles, in which one gamekeeper received minor injuries, the day continued as planned. However, on their jubilant return to Hayfield, the police were waiting and arrested a handful of the men, five, including Rothman, later being given custodial sentences at the Derby Assizes. But the cause now attracted a deal of public sympathy and there was outrage at the severity of the men's treatment. Disparate groups came together in a common cause, which ultimately received recognition in the enactment of the *National Park and Access to the Countryside Act* in 1949.

Soon becoming stepped, the path tackles the abrupt north western snout onto the plateau. Gaining the top, it then runs above a high scarp, aproned with a chaos of bouldery debris. There is a breathtaking view into the Kinder Valley, but that to the north is blocked by the rise of the bog, whose dark hags and deep groughs dissuade most people from venturing to explore the hinterland wilderness. Rounding a small promontory the cleft of the Kinder Downfall comes into sight and, on a shelf far below can be seen the small silvery tarn of the Mermaid's Pool. Carry on along the rim, eventually turning in above the Kinder Downfall to find a crossing point, well back from the edge **D**. Dependant upon the volume of water cascading off the plateau, the fall can be a spectacular sight and, when the prevailing wind blows in earnest, the updraft throws the water back in a white plume of spray. Veering south, the way returns to the edge, crossing another major stream, Red Brook, before the conspicuous cairn and trig point perched upon a boulder marking Kinder Low **E** appears.

One needs more than a good eye to find the high spots on the Kinder Scout plateau, a barely undulating blanket of bog that extends across some six square miles of desolate wilderness. The Ordnance Survey set three triangulation pillars on the hill during their survey: one north of the path on the approach to Kinder Downfall, another here and the third three miles to the east above Blackden Edge. Kinder Low at 2,077 feet (633m) is the most easily reached, but is not quite the greatest elevation. That honour goes to a bleak spot known simply as 'Point 636' (2,088 feet), which lies about $\frac{1}{2}$ mile to the north west at grid reference SK 085875 and marked by a forlorn pile of stones. Although not far, the groughs, hags and patches of cloying bog necessitate a wandering course across a demanding terrain and, with no landmarks, *it is easy to become disoriented*.

The main path runs a short distance west of the Kinder Low trig point past a large cairn. Leave it at that point, bearing east of south towards the prominent Edale Rocks. Beyond a small cairn an obvious trod develops, passing immediately left of the outcrop where a paved path suddenly begins. As the ground falls away a superb view opens along the deepening fold cradling the infant River Noe to the head of Edale, which is bounded at the far side by the long ridge centred on Mam Tor. To the east, the Kinder edge runs on past the outcrops of Noe Stool, Pym Chair and the sculpted boulders of the Wool Packs to Crowden Tower.

Reaching a junction marked by a large cairn, bear right, walking below the steepening face of Swine's Back. At the next fork, drop left with the main flagged path, but as that then swings left a little lower down, keep ahead to a signposted junction by a wall **F**. Turn right through a gate onto a broad, stony track that rises to a gate-gap topping the shoulder of the hill. Just beyond, tucked into a recess is the medieval Edale Cross, one of many stones of varying ages that marked the ancient pathways across the tops. The track then settles into a long and gradual descent off the moor, later marked to Hayfield via Coldwell Clough. Becoming metalled as it leaves the fell it drops through Coldwell Clough,

bending to meet a couple of gates. The footpath is signed to Hayfield via The Ashes through the right-hand gate, a field track dogging the stream. Later joining the metalled track from the farm it runs on to merge back with the lane.

Twist across a bridge **G** and follow the stream down to its confluence with the River Kinder by Bowden Bridge, a graceful structure from the days of the packhorse. Swing left with the lane, but when then it turns across the river, remain on the southern bank along a drive into the Camping and Caravanning Club Hayfield campsite. Keep ahead past the administration block on a riverside footpath. Reaching cottages the way becomes tarmacked

and leads into the village. Go right to the church, turning left in front of it back to the car park.

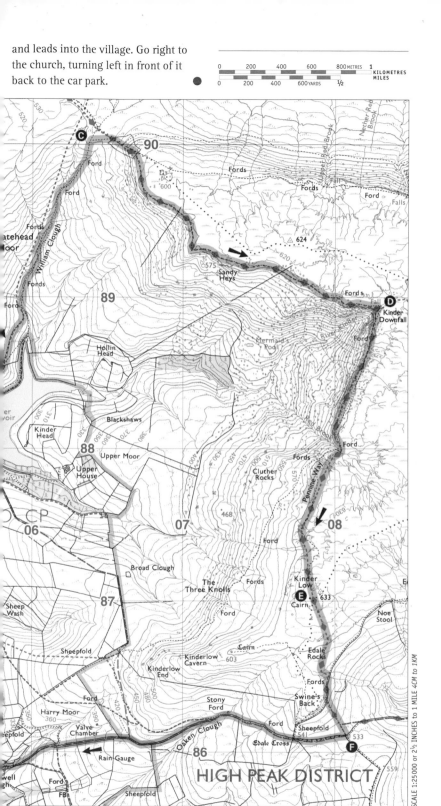

Margery Hill

		GPS waypoints	
Start	Fairholmes National Park Centre		SK 172 893
Distance	11¼ miles (18.1km)	**A**	SK 173 896
Height gain	2,000 feet (610m)	**B**	SK 169 951
Approximate time	5½ hours	**C**	SK 185 960
Parking	Car park at start (Pay and Display)	**D**	SK 189 956
Route terrain	Lakeside tracks and moorland paths, *good navigation skills required in mist*	**E**	SK 188 943
		F	SK 170 921
Ordnance Survey maps	Landranger 110 (Sheffield & Huddersfield), Explorer OL1 (The Peak District – Dark Peak area)		

The long preamble beside the Derwent and Howden reservoirs is a superb walk in itself and many folk would be satisfied to leave it at that. But carry on to climb out of Cranberry Clough onto Margery Hill and you are rewarded by some of the finest views in the whole of the Derwent Valley. The route meanders on at the rim of the high moor above a succession of rocky outcrops before gently descending along Howden Edge towards a deep valley biting far into the hill. After dropping through woods above Abbey Brook, the return retraces your outward steps beside the Derwent Reservoir. Inexperienced walkers are advised not to attempt the walk in poor visibility, for the hilltop path can be confusing in mist.

On Sundays, bank holidays and summer Saturdays, you can knock a couple of miles off the distance by taking the bus from Fairholmes to its terminus at King's Tree on the west bank of the Howden Reservoir. A track continues north beyond the head of the lake, crossing the River Derwent at Slippery Stones to meet the main route at Point **B***.*

A path to the dam leaves the car park by the National Park visitor centre. Joining the lane, follow it right below the dam but then, just beyond the bend, abandon the lane for a path that doubles back left **A**. Sloping uphill through a conifer plantation, it passes the end of the dam wall to meet a service track. The track meanders pleasantly north for four miles along the shores of the two lakes and then above the River Derwent, eventually reaching a junction of paths above a graceful packhorse bridge at Slippery Stones **B**. The 17th-century bridge originally crossed the river at the hamlet of Derwent, some 4½ miles to the south, and would have been flooded along with the village when the Ladybower Dam was completed in 1943. However, it was dismantled and eventually re-erected here in 1959 as a memorial to John Derry. Editor of the *Sheffield Daily Independent,* his walking features and subsequent book *Across the Derbyshire Moors* inspired many to explore the beautiful Peakland countryside.

Walk ahead, crossing a footbridge over Cranberry Brook and, at the next fork, go right, following the stream into the narrowing valley of Cranberry Clough. Immediately beyond a stream issuing from Bull Clough, bear left, climbing the abrupt spur that separates the two valleys. The gradient soon relents and the path settles to a steady plod, rising across the moor towards the distant Howden Edge. A sharp but short finale takes you up onto the rim, where a large cairn marks a faint crossing trod **Ⓒ**.

Turn off to the right, picking your way across the peaty moor towards a fence visible ahead on the skyline. It surrounds Margery Hill Cairn, a subtle mound in the heather that has been identified as a Bronze Age burial site. In the warmer climate of 3,500 years ago, these hill tops were extensively settled, the upland woods being cleared to create fields for agriculture and livestock. Beyond the enclosure, bear left from the edge to find a stile in a crossing fence. Keep the same line to reach a triangulation pillar marking the vague high point of the hill **Ⓓ**.

Despite the flat expanse to the east there is a 360° panorama of the distant horizon, with the high rise blocks of Sheffield, the Emley Moor and Holme Moss transmitters and the nearer wind farm on Spicer Hill all identifiable. The

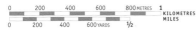

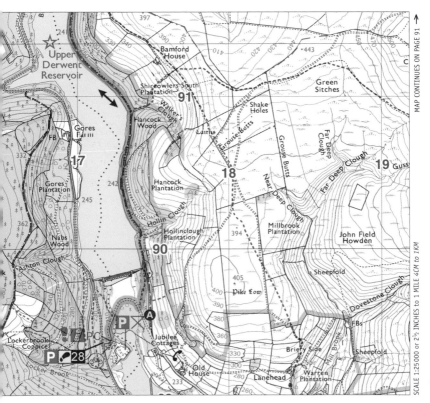

MAP CONTINUES ON PAGE 91 →

SCALE 1:25000 or 2½ INCHES to 1 MILE 4CM to 1KM

One of the Margery Stones

best views, however, are to be had from the edge, to which the onward path now tends between the curious natural forms of the Margery Stones. The path rambles on above the rim, where the eye is drawn across the deep fold of the Derwent Valley to the lonely hills beyond. Out to the west is Bleaklow and farther south are the Kinder plateau and the long Mam Tor ridge, while ahead the ground rises beckoningly to Lost Lad and Back Tor. The lakes below are initially obscured by the broad aprons of Upper Hey and Nether Hey, however, the changing perspective offers a glimpse to the Howden dam along the divide of Howden Clough.

Carry on above the edge for some ¾ mile, eventually arriving at a small cairn on top of High Stones **E**. Beyond there, the edge softens and the path tends left to fall beside a shallow, peaty gully. Ahead, a great rift opens, cleaving the mass of high ground and frustrating what had previously appeared a simple extension of the ridge walk onto Back Tor. Lower down, the path joins a developing shooters' track, which later curves right and drops more steeply towards the lower broad promontory shoulder of Nether Hey.

Reaching a fence, pass through a gate and bear left, watching for the grass track suddenly swinging left a little farther on and passing through more gates to the head of Cogman Clough. The way progresses west above the steep flank of the valley containing Abbey Brook, eventually leaving the moor through the intake wall. The descent continues across the sharp slope of Hey Bank, passing through sparse birch wood and then larch plantation before finally meeting the lakeside track **F**. The day ends with a leisurely stroll back above the Derwent Reservoir to Fairholmes. ●

Howden Reservoir

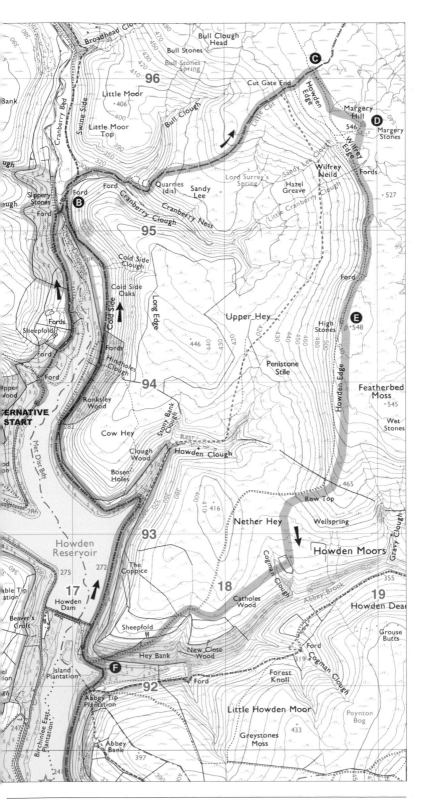

Further Information

Safety on the Hills

The hills, mountains and moorlands of Britain, though of modest height compared with those in many other countries, need to be treated with respect. Friendly and inviting in good weather, they can quickly be transformed into wet, misty, windswept and potentially dangerous areas of wilderness in bad weather. Even on an outwardly fine and settled summer day, conditions can rapidly deteriorate at high altitudes and, in winter, even more so.

Therefore it is advisable to always take both warm and waterproof clothing, sufficient nourishing food, a hot drink, first-aid kit, torch and whistle. Wear suitable footwear, such as strong walking-boots or shoes that give a good grip over rocky terrain and on slippery slopes. Try to obtain a local weather forecast and bear it in mind before you start. Do not be afraid to abandon your proposed route and return to your starting point in the event of a sudden and unexpected deterioration in the weather. Do not go alone and allow enough time to finish the walk well before nightfall.

Most of the walks described in this book do not venture into remote wilderness areas and will be safe to do, given due care and respect, at any time of year in all but the most unreasonable weather. Indeed, a crisp, fine winter day often provides perfect walking conditions, with firm ground underfoot and a clarity that is not possible to achieve in the other seasons of the year. A few walks, however, are suitable only for reasonably fit and experienced hill walkers able to use a compass and should definitely not be tackled by anyone else during the winter months or in bad weather, especially high winds and mist. These are indicated in the general description that precedes each of the walks.

Walkers and the Law

The Countryside and Rights of Way Act (CRoW Act 2000) extends the rights of access previously enjoyed by walkers in England and Wales. Implementation of these rights began on 19 September 2004. The Act amends existing legislation and for the first time provides access on foot to certain types of land – defined as mountain, moor, heath, down and registered common land.

Where You Can Go
Rights of Way
Prior to the introduction of the CRoW Act, walkers could only legally access the countryside along public rights of way. These are either 'footpaths' (for walkers only) or 'bridleways' (for walkers, riders on horseback and pedal cyclists). A third category called 'Byways open to all traffic' (BOATs), is used by motorised vehicles as well as those using non-mechanised transport. Mainly they are green lanes, farm and estate roads, although occasionally they will be found crossing mountainous area.

Rights of way are marked on Ordnance Survey maps. Look for the green broken lines on the Explorer maps, or the red dashed lines on Landranger maps.

The term 'right of way' means exactly what it says. It gives a right of passage over what, for the most part, is private land. Under pre-CRoW legislation walkers were required to keep to the line of the right of way and not stray onto land on either side. If you did inadvertently wander off the right of way, either because of faulty map reading or because the route was not clearly indicated on the ground, you were technically trespassing.

Local authorities have a legal obligation to ensure that rights of way are kept clear and free of obstruction, and are signposted where they leave metalled roads. The duty of local authorities to install signposts extends to the placing of signs along a path or way, but only where the authority considers it necessary to have a signpost or waymark to assist persons unfamiliar with the locality.

Countryside Access Charter

Your rights of way are:

- public footpaths – on foot only. Sometimes waymarked in yellow
- bridleways – on foot, horseback and pedal cycle. Sometimes waymarked in blue
- byways (usually old roads), most 'roads used as public paths' and, of course, public roads – all traffic has the right of way

Use maps, signs and waymarks to check rights of way. Ordnance Survey Explorer and Landranger maps show most public rights of way

On rights of way you can:

- take a pram, pushchair or wheelchair if practicable
- take a dog (on a lead or under close control)
- take a short route round an illegal obstruction or remove it sufficiently to get past

You have a right to go for recreation to:

- public parks and open spaces – on foot
- most commons near older towns and cities – on foot and sometimes on horseback
- private land where the owner has a formal agreement with the local authority

In addition you can use the following by local or established custom or consent, but ask for advice if you are unsure:

- many areas of open country, such as moorland, fell and coastal areas, especially those in the care of the National Trust, and some commons
- some woods and forests, especially those owned by the Forestry Commission
- country parks and picnic sites
- most beaches
- canal towpaths
- some private paths and tracks Consent sometimes extends to horse-riding and cycling

For your information:

- county councils and London boroughs maintain and record rights of way, and register commons
- obstructions, dangerous animals, harassment and misleading signs on rights of way are illegal and you should report them to the county council
- paths across fields can be ploughed, but must normally be reinstated within two weeks
- landowners can require you to leave land to which you have no right of access
- motor vehicles are normally permitted only on roads, byways and some 'roads used as public paths'

The New Access Rights
Access Land

As well as being able to walk on existing rights of way, under the new legislation you now have access to large areas of open land. You can of course continue to use rights of way footpaths to cross this land, but the main difference is that you can now lawfully leave the path and wander at will, but only in areas designated as access land.

Where to Walk

Areas now covered by the new access rights – Access Land – are shown on Ordnance

Survey Explorer maps bearing the access land symbol on the front cover.

'Access Land' is shown on Ordnance Survey maps by a light yellow tint surrounded by a pale orange border. New orange coloured 'i' symbols on the maps will show the location of permanent access information boards installed by the access authorities.

Restrictions

The right to walk on access land may lawfully be restricted by landowners. Landowners can, for any reason, restrict access for up to 28 days in any year. They cannot however close the land:

- on bank holidays;
- for more than four Saturdays and Sundays in a year;
- on any Saturday from 1 June to 11 August; or

Further Information

- on any Sunday from 1 June to the end of September.

They have to provide local authorities with five working days' notice before the date of closure unless the land involved is an area of less than five hectares or the closure is for less than four hours. In these cases land-owners only need to provide two hours' notice.

Whatever restrictions are put into place on access land they have no effect on existing rights of way, and you can continue to walk on them.

Dogs

Dogs can be taken on access land, but must be kept on leads of two metres or less between 1 March and 31 July, and at all times where they are near livestock. In addition landowners may impose a ban on all dogs from fields where lambing takes place for up to six weeks in any year. Dogs may be banned from moorland used for grouse shooting and breeding for up to five years.

In the main, walkers following the routes in this book will continue to follow existing rights of way, but a knowledge and understanding of the law as it affects walkers, plus the ability to distinguish access land marked on the maps, will enable anyone who wishes to depart from paths that cross access land either to take a shortcut, to enjoy a view or to explore.

General Obstructions

Obstructions can sometimes cause a problem on a walk and the most common of these is where the path across a field has been ploughed over. It is legal for a farmer to plough up a path provided that it is restored within two weeks. This does not always happen and you are faced with the dilemma of following the line of the path, even if this means treading on crops, or walking round the edge of the field. Although the later course of action seems the most sensible, it does mean that you would be trespassing.

Other obstructions can vary from overhanging vegetation to wire fences across the path, locked gates or even a cattle feeder on the path.

Use common sense. If you can get round the obstruction without causing damage, do so. Otherwise only remove as much of the obstruction as is necessary to secure passage.

If the right of way is blocked and cannot be followed, there is a long-standing view that in such circumstances there is a right to deviate, but this cannot wholly be relied on. Although it is accepted in law that highways (and that includes rights of way) are for the public service, and if the usual track is impassable, it is for the general good that people should be entitled to pass into another line. However, this should not be taken as indicating a right to deviate whenever a way becomes impassable. If in doubt, retreat.

Report obstructions to the local authority and/or the Ramblers' Association.

 ## Useful Organisations

Campaign to Protect Rural England
128 Southwark Street,
London SE1 0SW
Tel. 020 7981 2800
www.cpre.org.uk

Camping and Caravanning Club
Greenfields House, Westwood Way,
Coventry CV4 8JH
Site bookings Tel. 0845 130 7633
www.campingandcaravanningclub.co.uk

Council for National Parks
6-7 Barnard Mews, London SW11 1QU
Tel. 020 7924 4077
www.cnp.org.uk

English Heritage
PO Box 569, Swindon, Wiltshire SN2 2YP
Tel. 0870 333 1181
www.english-heritage.org.uk

Forestry Commission
Silvan House, 231 Corstorphine Road,
Edinburgh EH12 7AT
Tel. 0131 334 0303
www.forestry.gov.uk

Friends of the Peak District
'The Stables', 22a Endcliffe Crescent,
Sheffield S10 3EF
Tel. 0114 266 5822
www.friendsofthepeak.org.uk

National Trust
Membership and general enquiries
PO Box 39, Warrington WA5 7WD
Tel. 0844 800 1895
www.nationaltrust.org.uk
East Midlands Regional Office
Clumber Park Stableyard, Worksop,
Nottinghamshire S80 3BE
Tel. 01909 486411

Natural England
1 East Parade, Sheffield
S1 2ET
Tel. 0114 241 8920
www.naturalengland.org.uk

Ordnance Survey
Romsey Road, Southampton
SO16 4GU
Tel. 08456 05 05 05
www.ordnancesurvey.co.uk

Peak and Northern Footpaths Society
Taylor House, 23 Turncroft Lane,
Offerton, Stockport
SK1 4AB
Tel. 0161 480 3565
www.peakandnorthern.org.uk

Peak District National Park Authority
Aldern House, Baslow Road,
Bakewell, Derbyshire DE45 1AE
Tel. 01629 816200
www.peakdistrict.org

Peak District Information Centres
Bakewell
Old Market Hall, Bridge Street,
Bakewell, Derbyshire DE45 1DS
Tel. 01629 816558

Castleton
Buxton Road, Castleton, Hope Valley
S33 8WN
Tel. 01629 816572

The Moorland Centre, Edale
Fieldhead, Edale, Hope Valley S33 7ZA
Tel. 01443 670207

Upper Derwent
Fairholmes, Bamford, Hope Valley
S33 0AQ
Tel. 01433 650953

Ramblers' Association
2nd Floor, Camelford House,
87-90 Albert Embankment,
London SE1 7TW
Tel. 020 7339 8500
www.ramblers.org.uk

Visit Peak District & Derbyshire
Crescent View, Hall Bank, Buxton,
Derbyshire SK17 6EN
Tel. 0845 833 0970
www.visitpeakdistrict.com

Tourist information centres:
Ashbourne: Tel: 01335 343666
Bakewell: Tel: 01629 816558
Buxton: Tel: 01298 25106
Castleton: Tel: 01629 816558
Glossop: Tel: 01457 869176
Leek: Tel: 01538 483741
Manifold Valley: Tel: 01298 84679
Matlock: Tel: 01629 583388
Saddleworth: Tel: 01457 870336
The Moorland Centre: Tel: 01433 670207
Upper Derwent Valley: Tel: 01433 650953

Youth Hostels Association
Trevelyan House, Dimple Road,
Matlock, Derbyshire DE4 3YH
Tel. 01629 592600
www.yha.org.uk

 Ordnance Survey maps of the Peak District

The Peak District is covered by Ordnance Survey 1:50 000 scale (1¼ inches to 1 mile or 2cm to 1km) Landranger sheets 109, 110, 118 and 119. These all-purpose maps are packed with information to help you explore the area. Viewpoints, picnic sites, places of interest, caravan and camping sites are shown, as well as public rights of way information such as footpaths and bridleways.

To examine the Peak District in more detail, and especially if you are planning walks, Ordnance Survey Explorer maps at 1:25 000 (2½ inches to 1 mile or 4cm to 1km) scale are ideal.

OL1 – The Peak District (Dark Peak area)
OL24 – The Peak District (White Peak area)
OL21 – South Pennines

To get to the Peak District, use the Ordnance Survey OS Travel Map–Route Great Britain at 1:625 000 scale (1 inch to 10 miles or 4cm to 25km) or Road Map 4 (Northern England) at 1:250 000 scale (1 inch to 4 miles or 1cm to 2.5km).

Ordnance Survey maps and guides are available from most booksellers, stationers and newsagents.

Further Information

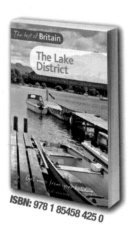